FRESH
mob

FRESH

mob

Over 100 tasty, healthy-ish recipes

Photography by David Loftus

HODDER & STOUGHTON

BRUNCH

HEARTY

SPEEDY

FRESHEST

WEEKEND

SHARING

SUMMERY

PUDDINGS

Welcome to *Fresh Mob*. This is the book that you're going to cook from time and time again – a soon to be dog-eared kitchen classic packed full of the freshest bangers for every occasion.

This cookbook is an evolution of Mob. You spoke, we listened, and we've created an entire cookbook of recipes that focus on the good stuff without compromising on flavour. Don't get us wrong, we're big fans of indulgence every now and again, but life's all about balance. And nothing beats the satisfaction of eating something that's super-tasty which just also happens to be good for you. As a team, that's the sort of food we cook on a day-to-day basis. Because as much as we do love a carbonara, having it every day of the week would probably be overkill.

Another reason we wanted to write this cookbook was that we hadn't seen anything like it on the shelves. Let's be frank: a good majority of the 'healthy food' market demonizes food, is often all about body image or gender, and ultimately focuses on failure and shame rather than actually offering you any genuine help. This cookbook is going to change that.

Fresh food is as much about making a quick meal after a hectic day at work that warms you up from the inside as it is about eating a dish that transports you to your summer holiday or making a sharing feast that you can tuck into with your Mob. It's vibrant, it's colourful and it's the food that you crave after a big weekend.

Working alongside nutritionist Lucy Sommer, we've established our own Fresh Criteria with a focus on balanced eating and flexibility at its core. This, for us, is a much more realistic and honest stance on how people really eat. We know that sometimes wholemeal bread just won't cut it and that some crusty ciabatta rolls are exactly what you're after. We get you – because we think the same thing. Life's too short not to eat pasta. We're not here to tell you how to live your life, we're just trying to help make it more delicious.

So, what's changed?

Not a huge amount, to be honest. We've still included all the things we know you love, but we've come up with clever ways of including all of our favourite ingredients in smaller quantities that don't mean sacrificing on flavour or enjoyment. Think using an 'nduja and garlic spiced butter to deliver a burst of flavour in a small package, or making less feta go further by lightening it with lemony Greek yoghurt.

As always, our recipes are built to satisfy. You may notice that we've used fewer carbs than in previous cookbooks, but that's not because we're suddenly looking to give you meagre portion sizes, or because we think carbs are 'bad'. We've just bulked out the recipes with heaps of veggies and lean protein in order to achieve a balanced plate that'll fill you up.

We've opted for healthier cooking methods wherever possible, too. Take our epic miso chicken schnitzel with kimchi mayo as a case study. Baking that schnitzel over a wire rack, rather than frying it, ensures that you get all of the crisp without any of the oil. It's an easy win that makes the dish lighter without jeopardizing its integrity.

The Fresh Plate

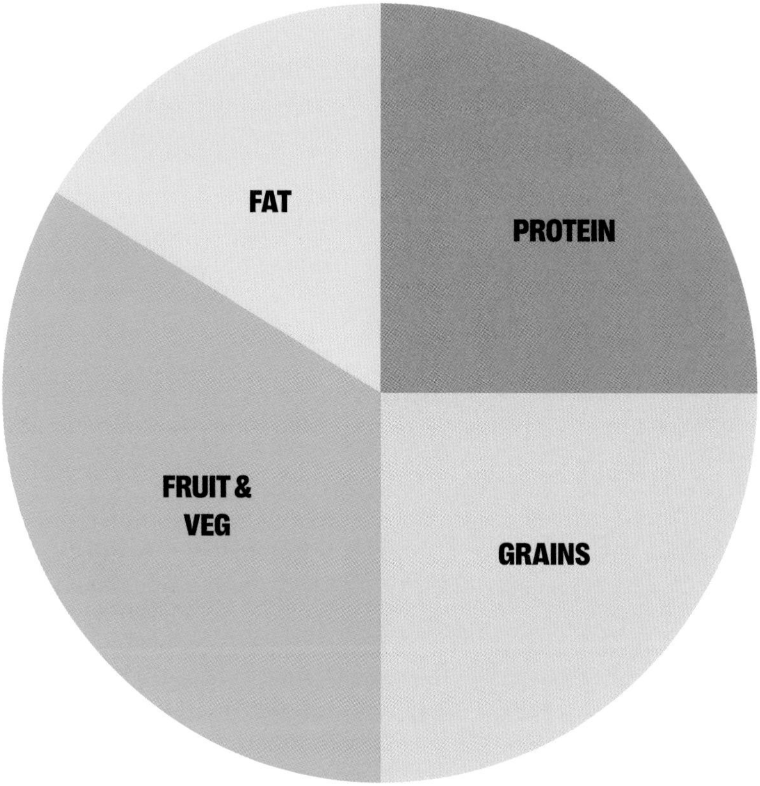

Protein – Important for muscle growth and repair, protein also keeps us fuller for longer by balancing our blood sugar and insulin levels. [*Infographic: 25% of the plate*]

Carbohydrates – Our main energy source, found in all fruit, vegetables, grains, nuts, pulses and seeds.

Grains and starchy vegetables – Made up of sugar and starch, which are turned into glucose and used as energy. They are also an excellent source of B vitamins and minerals. [*Infographic: 25% of the plate*]

Non-starchy vegetables and fruit – Contain plenty of micronutrients which are vital for good health and disease prevention. They also contain high amounts of fibre, which is essential for digestion and good gut health. [*Infographic: 40–50% of the plate*]

Fat – An essential macronutrient that has numerous functions in the body. Unsaturated fats in the form of healthy oils, avocados and nuts and seeds are especially great as they can help support immunity and reduce the risk of heart disease. [*Infographic: 5–10% of the plate*]

And if you're not fussed about things being a bit fresher? Well, you do you. Just sit back, relax and enjoy this cookbook for the 10/10 recipes it includes without worrying about whether or not your dinner contains any antioxidants. Or worrying about what antioxidants even are, for that matter.

When we think of fresh food, there's a list of characteristics that come to mind and we've worked hard to make sure each recipe nails at least one of these categories:

Zingy You know that moment where your whole mouth is filled with a lasting flavour that you can't get enough of? That's what we're talking about when we say something's zingy. Think roasted aubergine and butternut salad with an umami XO dressing or our blood orange and sea bass tostadas, the corn tortilla cleverly baked in the oven rather than fried.

Crunchy What is it about eating something crunchy that just makes you feel alive? We don't know the exact science behind it, but we do know that we've got a rainbow-coloured tofu salad with the creamiest miso and tahini dressing that proves just how important texture is to a meal. Crispy and crunchy is the best way to eat tofu.

Warming Sometimes you need something a bit heartier for your dinner – something to hug you from the inside out. For those days when you're craving something warming that won't make you uncomfortably full, we've got you covered. Sophie's got a curry leaf and peanut chicken curry that's ready in 30 minutes. And if that doesn't float your boat, try our hot sauce and corn gnocchi. Or our meatball macaroni soup. Or our orzo with broccoli and pumpkin seed pesto with fried garlic and anchovies. The options are endless.

Wholesome Like warming, but a tad lighter. Seema's lemon and olive braised chicken hits all the right spots with its briny, citrusy flavour profile. Other wholesome classics like our squash dal with broccoli tarka, aubergine dhansak with coriander yoghurt and tahini broth noodles should also satisfy your stomach and soul in a similar manner.

Herby Herbs are packed full of nutrients and elevate practically any dish you put them in, which is why we've included them in near enough every recipe in this cookbook. For a herbaceous showstopper, try Jordon's roasted celeriac with muhammara and herby salad. It's a must-eat.

Light Sometimes you want to eat a meal and still be able to do something energetic afterwards, like go to the gym or take your dog for a walk around the park. Our green udon with blitzed avo and cashew dressing and sesame chilli-crusted fish with zesty tomato salad are just two examples of recipes for those occasions. This cookbook is filled with many, many more.

Toppers and twists It was very important for us that all the recipes in this book are exciting. That's why you'll notice more toppers, twists and flavour-packed sauces than ever before. We're talking along the lines of curried roast broccoli with turmeric yoghurt and shallot peanut dressing, a grilled chicken burger with mojo verde and jalapeño salsa, our soon-to-be-famous gochujang egg mayo, and 'nduja Turkish eggs.

Something sweet We've all naturally got a bit of a sweet tooth. We wanted to include some puds that were capable of deliciously capping off the end of a great meal but weren't packed with sugar. We've got a vegan ice cream simply made from blitzed frozen bananas that we've served with a homemade chocolate hazelnut sauce, some surprising secret-ingredient brownies, and the tastiest-ever clementine almond cake made using olive oil.

It's important to us that you can easily find the recipes that you're looking for, which is why we've included these icons throughout:

Vegan/Vegetarian *Fresh Mob* features more vegan and veggie recipes than ever. The way we see it, food that's better for the planet is generally better for you too.

Gluten-Free/Dairy-Free We're all about inclusivity and have included an icon for when our recipes are gluten-free or dairy-free to help you easily navigate any dietary requirements.

Under 30 minutes We know you want good food fast. That's why we've dedicated a whole chapter to speedy recipes and included this helpful timer throughout the book to indicate which recipes you should have a go at when you're pushed for time.

V Veggie

VG Vegan

GF Gluten-free

DF Dairy-free

30 Under 30 Minutes

We know we say this every time, but this really is our best book to date, mainly due to the simple fact that you were the ones who inspired it; *Fresh Mob* was created because it was something that you all asked us for. It celebrates everything we love about cooking and eating, and we can't wait to see all your re-creations at home. We hope you enjoy eating these dishes as much as we enjoyed making them.

Ben and the whole Mob team x

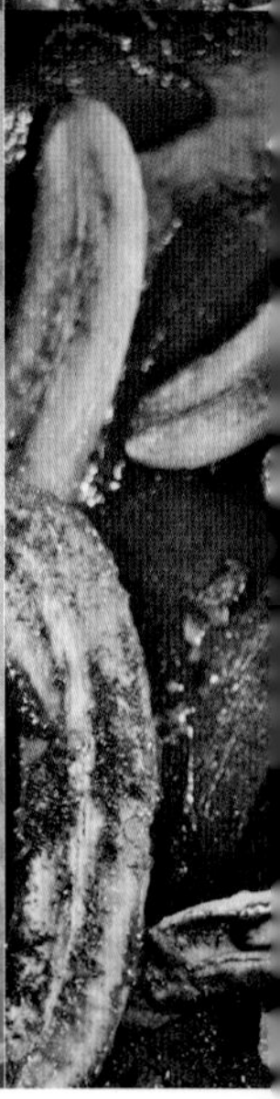

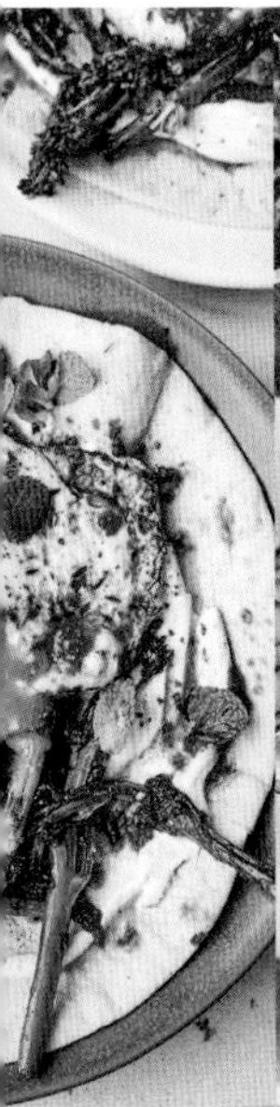

BRUNCH

Chilli Jam Broccoli *& Yoghurt* **Flatbreads**

Chilli jam is one of those ingredients that you buy on a whim and then start putting on everything. This speedy brunch is sure to become a firm favourite. As for the combination of glazed, charred broccoli with a cumin seed fried egg – what's not to love?

Cook time: 25 mins

Ingredients

Serves 4

400g (4oz) tenderstem broccoli
2 tbsp olive oil
3 tbsp chilli jam, plus a drizzle to serve
4 medium eggs
2 tsp cumin seeds
4 large flatbreads
200g (7oz) Greek yoghurt
½ tsp chilli flakes
a handful of mint leaves

Gluten-Free: Make sure you use gluten-free bread.

Method

1. Get a kettle on to boil. Cut any larger tenderstem florets in half lengthways.

2. Pour the water into your largest saucepan over a high heat and add salt. Once the water returns to the boil, drop in the broccoli. Cook for 1 minute – set a timer, you don't want to cook the broccoli fully, just take the edge off. Drain into a colander, then leave to steam-dry for a couple of minutes.

3. Get a large frying pan over a super-high heat. Pour in ½ tablespoon of the olive oil, lay in half the broccoli, season and fry, turning throughout until charred in places. Tip onto a plate and repeat with another ½ tablespoon of oil and the remaining broccoli. Once all the broccoli is charred, tip it all back into the pan over a low heat, add the chilli jam, toss together and keep warm.

4. Get a second frying pan over a high heat and pour in the remaining tablespoon of olive oil. Crack in the eggs, then sprinkle over the cumin seeds. Fry to your liking.

5. Warm the flatbreads, then spread the Greek yoghurt over them. Divide the broccoli between each flatbread and top with a cumin fried egg, chilli flakes, mint leaves and a drizzle more chilli jam to serve. Banging.

Marinated Peppers *on* **Toast**

V GF

The star of the show here is the homemade charred, marinated peppers – just like the ones from the jar, but a thousand times better. Using a combination of colourful peppers boosts the number of phytonutrients, which are great for reducing the risk of chronic disease. Tossed in vinegar, capers, olive oil and chilli flakes, these peppers make a statement when served on top of creamy ricotta and crunchy sourdough.

Cook time: 1 hr (including the agonizing wait!)

Ingredients

Serves 4

- 6 mixed peppers (we love a combination of orange, yellow and red)
- 1 small garlic clove
- 3 tbsp olive oil
- 1 tsp chilli flakes, plus a sprinkle to serve
- 2 tbsp capers
- 2–3 tbsp sherry vinegar (depending on how sharp you like it – get the best quality you can afford here)
- 3 tbsp pine nuts
- 8 slices of sourdough
- 200g (7oz) ricotta
- a small handful of basil leaves
- salt and black pepper

Gluten-Free: Make sure you use gluten-free bread.

Cooking Hack: If you have a gas hob you can also blacken the peppers directly over the flame for some added smoky char.

Method

1. Preheat the grill to high.

2. Put the whole peppers onto a large baking tray, season with salt and pepper, then slide under the grill, turning every 5 minutes until the outsides are blackened in places and they have collapsed and softened – this will take about 20 minutes. Leave to cool slightly in a bowl (they will continue to soften).

3. Once the peppers are cool enough to handle, peel away most of the blackened skin – don't worry about a few bits as this will just add to the flavour. Remove the seeds and stalk and then thickly slice.

4. Put the peppers into a clean bowl. Strain over any of their cooking liquid (you don't want any seeds) then crush in the garlic, add the olive oil, chilli flakes, capers and enough sherry vinegar according to your taste. Season and set aside to marinate. If you can do this the day before and keep in the fridge, great; if not, 20 minutes at room temperature will be fine.

5. Meanwhile, toast the pine nuts in a small dry frying pan over a medium heat until golden – watch closely as they can suddenly turn.

6. When you are ready to eat, toast the sourdough, then spread over the ricotta. Spoon over the peppers, along with the capers and juices, and crack over some black pepper. Scatter over some chilli flakes and tear over the basil leaves to serve.

Roasted *Asparagus* **with Gribiche**

V GF DF 30

Sauce gribiche is a French classic, and a fancy word for what is effectively a pimped-up egg mayo that's been spiked with mustard, vinegar, parsley, cornichons and capers. We've added almonds to make it more robust and nutritious. You can't beat it when it's with some simple roasted asparagus. Or should that be *asperges*?

Cook time: 25 mins

Ingredients

Serves 4

400g (14oz) asparagus
3 tbsp olive oil
8 medium eggs
50g (1¾oz) smoked or roasted and salted almonds
8 cornichons
2 tbsp capers
a small bunch of parsley
2–3 tsp Dijon mustard, to taste
2 tbsp white wine vinegar
4 large slices of sourdough
salt and black pepper

Gluten-Free: Make sure you use gluten-free bread.

Ingredient Hack: If asparagus isn't in season, swap for the same amount of tenderstem or purple sprouting broccoli instead. Use the asparagus ends, finely chopped, in a risotto or spring stew.

Method

1. Preheat the oven to 200°C/180°C fan/gas mark 6. Get a saucepan of water on to boil.

2. Snap the woody ends off the asparagus and tip into your largest roasting tin. Toss with 1 tablespoon of the olive oil and plenty of seasoning, then spread into a single layer so that they roast evenly. Roast in the oven for 10–12 minutes until the asparagus is just tender; set aside.

3. Meanwhile, lower the eggs into the pan of water and cook for 7 minutes – set a timer as you want them just set with the hint of a jammy centre.

4. Roughly chop the almonds and set aside. Finely chop the cornichons, capers and parsley (stalks and all).

5. Once the eggs are cooked, drain, briefly run under cold water to cool, then peel. Put into a large bowl and use a fork to mash into small pieces. Add the mustard, vinegar and remaining 2 tablespoons of olive oil and mash again, then add the cornichons, capers and parsley. Fold together and season to taste. Sauce gribiche done.

6. Toast the bread. Top with the asparagus and sauce gribiche, then scatter over the almonds to serve.

'Nduja *Turkish* Eggs

GF · 30

Nail your next brunch with this riff on a Turkish çılbır. Charred Padrón peppers are tossed in smoked paprika and salt, while lemony Greek yoghurt forms the base for quick pickled onions, runny poached eggs and a garlicky 'nduja butter. It's a belter.

Cook time: 30 minutes

Ingredients

Serves 4

1 small red onion
1 lemon
200g (7oz) Greek yoghurt
100g (3½oz) 'nduja
2 tbsp olive oil
2 fat garlic cloves
8 medium eggs
260g (9oz) Padrón peppers
2 tsp smoked paprika
a small handful of parsley
salt and black pepper
sliced focaccia, sourdough or flatbreads, to serve

Gluten-Free: Make sure you use gluten-free bread.

Method

1. Very finely chop the red onion and tip into a small bowl. Zest the lemon onto a plate and set aside, then squeeze the juice over the red onion, season with a big pinch of salt, stir and set aside.

2. Stir most of the lemon zest into the Greek yoghurt and season with salt and pepper.

3. Get a large saucepan of water on to boil.

4. Meanwhile, put the 'nduja and 1 tablespoon of the olive oil into a small saucepan over a medium–high heat. Use the back of your spoon to smoosh the 'nduja and encourage it to melt. Once melted, crush in the garlic cloves and cook for 30 seconds, then turn the heat to super-low so that the 'nduja just stays warm.

5. Poached egg time. Control the heat on your saucepan of water, so that the water is at a rolling boil. Use the top of your spoon to create a whirlpool effect. Crack 2 of the eggs into the pan, as close to the water as possible. Cook for 3–4 minutes until the white is set and the yolk is still runny. Use a slotted spoon to transfer to kitchen paper to drain. Repeat with the remaining eggs.

6. In between poaching the eggs, fry the Padrón peppers. Get a large non-stick frying pan super-hot. Once nearly smoking, add the peppers, along with the remaining tablespoon of olive oil. Fry, turning regularly, until blackened in places, collapsed and softened – this takes about 5 minutes. Tip into a bowl, stir in the smoked paprika and season well with salt and pepper.

7. Assembly time. Spread the Greek yoghurt across the base of four plates, then divide the Padrón peppers equally over the top. Place two poached eggs on top, season, then spoon over the 'nduja and finely chopped red onion. Tear over the parsley leaves and top with the remaining lemon zest. Serve with bread of your choice, for mopping.

Kimchi *& Cheddar* **Omurice**

***Omurice* is a Japanese omelette filled with fried rice. Our fresh take uses cooked rice mixed with veg, kimchi (which helps gut bacteria flourish) and grated Cheddar for a big medley of large flavours. You'll notice this recipe only serves two because it's better to make omelettes one at a time.**

Cook time: 30 mins

Ingredients

Serves 2

- 75g (2¾oz) basmati rice
- 40g (1½oz) extra-mature Cheddar cheese
- 1 carrot
- 2 spring onions
- a small handful of coriander
- 100g (3½oz) kimchi
- 4 large eggs
- 2 tsp soy sauce
- 2 tsp sesame oil
- 2 tsp crispy chilli oil (we like Lee Kum Kee)
- salt and black pepper

Gluten-Free: Check the label on the kimchi and use tamari instead of soy sauce.

Speed Hack: To cut the cooking time in half, simply use 150g (5½oz) pre-cooked rice and start the recipe at step 2.

Method

1. Cook the rice according to the packet instructions.

2. Meanwhile, coarsely grate the Cheddar into a small bowl. Peel the carrot into long ribbons, thinly slice the spring onions (both green and white parts) and the coriander stalks.

3. Once the rice is cooked, mix through the spring onions, carrot, coriander stalks and 2 tablespoons of juice from the kimchi. Season to taste.

4. Omelette time. It may feel tedious but the best way to do this is one at a time. Crack 2 of the eggs into a jug, add 1 teaspoon of soy sauce and whisk well until the whites and yolks are fully combined.

5. Get a small non-stick frying pan over a medium heat. Pour in 1 teaspoon of sesame oil, use a piece of kitchen paper to spread it across the base of the pan, then pour in your beaten egg.

6. Leave to cook for about 30 seconds until the edges begin to set, then using a spatula, drag some of the outside cooked egg into the centre of the pan, letting some of the raw egg run to the outside. Do this a couple of times until the egg is mostly set, then spoon half the rice, kimchi and grated Cheddar onto one side of the omelette. Using a spatula, flip the empty half over the filling. Cook for 30 seconds more to melt the cheese, then slide onto a plate.

7. Repeat the process for the second omelette – hopefully you have a nice friend who will wait to eat with you. To serve, tear over the coriander leaves and drizzle with crispy chilli oil.

Herby Feta *Scrambled* Eggs

V GF 30

This is an incredibly simple, fresh twist on scrambled eggs that uses one of our favourite ingredients: feta. A variety of fresh herbs help to boost the nutritional profile of this simple staple, making breakfast that much healthier. The key, as it always is with eggs, is not to overcook them. Feel free to swap out the dill for another herb like coriander.

Cook time: 10 mins

Ingredients

Serves 2

30g (1oz) butter
2 garlic cloves
30g (1oz) parsley
30g (1oz) dill
6 medium eggs
100g (3½oz) feta
1 tsp smoked paprika
olive oil, for drizzling
wholegrain or seeded toast, to serve

Gluten-Free: Make sure you use gluten-free bread.

Method

1. Place a non-stick frying pan over a medium–low heat and add the butter. Thinly slice the garlic, add to the pan and cook gently for about 2 minutes until softened but not browned.

2. Meanwhile, finely chop all of the herbs and set aside.

3. Lightly beat the eggs in a bowl and stir in three-quarters of the herbs. Pour into the pan and crumble in three-quarters of the feta. Cook gently while stirring all the time until the mixture is just set – you want soft, silky curds.

4. Plate up, or pop straight on top of some toast. Finish with the remaining herbs and feta, the smoked paprika and a good drizzle of olive oil.

Sweet Potato *& Halloumi* **Sandwich**

V GF 30

This has all the makings of the perfect veggie sandwich. Softened, caramelized shallots and hearty chunks of sweet potato get along famously with salty halloumi, crunchy lettuce and the chilli tang of chimichurri. Top of its class.

Cook time: 30 mins

Ingredients

Serves 4

1 large sweet potato
2½ banana shallots
4 tbsp olive oil
1½ tsp dried oregano
1 tbsp cumin seeds
½–1 red chilli (depending on how spicy you like it)
a small bunch of parsley
1 garlic clove
1–2 tbsp red wine vinegar (depending on how sharp you like it)
250g (9oz) pack of halloumi
1 baby gem lettuce
4 ciabatta rolls
salt and black pepper

Gluten-Free: Make sure you use gluten-free bread.

Method

1. Preheat the oven to 220°C/200°C fan/gas mark 7.

2. Leaving the skin on, cut the potatoes into roughly 1cm (½in) rounds. Peel and halve 2 of the shallots lengthways. Put the potatoes and shallots into a large roasting tin, toss with 1 tablespoon of the olive oil, 1 teaspoon of dried oregano, the cumin seeds and plenty of seasoning, then spread roughly into a single layer so that everything roasts evenly. Roast in the oven for 20 minutes, flipping halfway, until soft and a little caramelized.

3. Meanwhile, make the chimichurri. Finely chop the remaining shallot half and the red chilli and scrape into a small bowl. Finely chop the parsley (stalks and all), add to the bowl, then crush in the garlic clove. Add the remaining ½ teaspoon of dried oregano, 3 tablespoons of olive oil, the vinegar and 2 tablespoons of water. Stir and season to taste.

4. Once the veg is roasted, set aside to cool a little while you fry the halloumi. Cut the halloumi into thick slices and get a non-stick frying pan over a medium–high heat. Add the halloumi and fry until deeply golden, about 2 minutes on each side.

5. Assembly time. Roughly tear the lettuce leaves. Halve the ciabatta rolls and spread the bottom of each roll with a little chimichurri. Layer in the roasted veg, halloumi and torn lettuce leaves, then spoon over any remaining chimichurri and sandwich together. A veggie sandwich dream.

Herb Fritters *with Poached Eggs* **& Sumac Salad**

V GF

This is the brunch you make for people you want to impress. The herby fritters packed full of pumpkin seeds (a great source of unsaturated fats) and spices are already legit in their own right, so just imagine how good they get when they're topped with runny poached eggs, cooling yoghurt and a tomato sumac salad.

Cook time: 40 mins

Ingredients

Serves 4

75g (2¾oz) pumpkin seeds
1 red onion
1 red chilli
a small bunch each of parsley, dill and coriander
75g (2¾oz) fresh breadcrumbs
3 tsp sumac
2 tsp ground cumin, plus a pinch
2 tsp ground coriander, plus a pinch
8 large eggs
3 tbsp olive oil
4 tsp white wine vinegar
200g (7oz) cherry tomatoes
150g (5½oz) natural yoghurt
salt and black pepper

Gluten-Free: Make sure you use gluten-free breadcrumbs.

Method

1. Toast the pumpkin seeds in a dry frying pan over a medium heat until beginning to pop and turn golden. Set aside to cool.

2. Finely chop the red onion and chilli. Divide between two separate bowls. Finely chop two-thirds of the herbs (stalks and all) and add to one of the bowls. Tear the remaining herbs into the other bowl, then set the bowl of torn herbs aside for the salad later.

3. Add the breadcrumbs, 1 teaspoon of the sumac and 2 teaspoons each of the ground coriander and cumin to the bowl of chopped herbs. Tip in around three-quarters of the pumpkin seeds and season everything generously with salt and pepper, then crack in 4 of the eggs. Beat together until a batter forms. Set aside for 5 minutes to thicken.

4. Meanwhile, preheat the oven to 120°C/100°C fan/gas mark ½. Get a deep saucepan of water on to boil.

5. Get a large non-stick frying pan over a medium–high heat. Pour in 1 tablespoon of the olive oil, then using half the mix, spoon 4 fritters into the pan. Fry for 2 minutes on each side until set and deeply golden brown. Transfer to a roasting tin and repeat with the remaining batter and 1 tablespoon of oil, then transfer to the oven to keep warm.

6. Poached egg time. Pour 1 teaspoon of vinegar into the saucepan and adjust the heat so that the water is at a rolling boil. Use the top of your spoon to create a whirlpool effect. Crack 2 of the eggs into the pan, as close to the water as possible. Cook for 3–4 minutes until the white is set and the yolk is still runny. Drain with a slotted spoon onto kitchen paper. Repeat with the remaining 2 eggs.

7. Between poaching the eggs make the salad. Halve the cherry tomatoes, add to the bowl of torn herbs along with the remaining sumac and a pinch of ground coriander and cumin. Tip in the remaining pumpkin seeds, then pour in 1 tablespoon of olive oil and remaining 3 teaspoons of vinegar. Toss and season to taste.

8. Divide the fritters between four plates and spoon over the yoghurt. Top with the poached eggs and the tomato sumac salad to serve. Freshness personified.

Gochujang Egg *Mayo* **Toasts**

V DF 30

Everyone's done an egg mayo but no one's ever done it with gochujang. Until now, that is. That moreish red chilli paste adds a funk and spice to the classic base. We've even gone a step further by adding sesame-fried cabbage for an extra nutritional boost plus some quick-pickled cucumber.

Cook time: 30 mins

Ingredients

Serves 4

8 medium eggs
½ cucumber
1 small garlic clove
3½ tbsp rice wine vinegar
3 tbsp sesame seeds
1 small hispi cabbage (also known as sweetheart or pointed cabbage in the supermarket)
4 tbsp mayonnaise
1½ tbsp gochujang
1½ tbsp sesame oil
4 large thick slices of bread (we like a crusty granary or cob)
salt and black pepper

Method

1. Get a saucepan of water on to boil. Once boiling, lower in the eggs and set a timer for 7½ minutes – you want the eggs just hard-boiled.

2. Meanwhile, cut the cucumber into matchsticks. Put into a small bowl, finely grate over the garlic, then pour over 2 tablespoons of the rice wine vinegar. Season and set aside to quick-pickle.

3. Next, toast the sesame seeds in a large dry frying pan over a medium heat until turning golden. Leave to cool a little, then scrape into a bowl. Very thinly slice the cabbage.

4. Come back to the eggs: drain and rinse them until cool, then peel. Put into a bowl and mash with a fork. Add the mayonnaise and gochujang and mash again to combine, then season to taste. Set aside.

5. Get the same frying pan back over a high heat (no need to wash in between!). Add the cabbage and dry-fry for a couple of minutes until the cabbage begins to wilt and char. Pour in the sesame oil and cook for a couple minutes more until softened, then add the remaining 1½ tablespoons of rice wine vinegar and most of the toasted sesame seeds. Stir and season to taste.

6. Assembly time: toast the bread and then spoon over the sesame cabbage. Top with the egg mayo and then finally the pickled cucumbers and a sprinkling of toasted sesame seeds. Marvel at the beauty, then eat.

SPEEDY

Mushroom *& Lemongrass Soup* **with Spicy Oil**

VG GF DF 30

This dairy-free soup is a beautiful thing. It's packed with aromatics like lemongrass, ginger and garlic, then topped with crispy mushrooms and an incredible spicy oil. We added heaps of mushrooms, which are full of micronutrients such as B vitamins. Suitable for any occasion you can think of.

Cook time: 30 mins

Ingredients

Serves 4

8 spring onions
750g (1lb 10oz) chestnut mushrooms
2 lemongrass stalks
2cm (¾in) piece of fresh ginger
3 garlic cloves
1 medium potato
2 tbsp vegetable oil
1 × 400ml (14fl oz) tin of coconut milk
700ml (1¼ pints) vegetable stock
1 tsp chilli flakes
salt and black pepper

Cooking Hack: Make sure your mushrooms are extra crispy: this may take a few extra minutes but it's so worth it for that crunch.

Gluten-Free: Use gluten-free stock.

Method

1. Dice up the spring onions, separating the whites and the greens. Cut 300g (10½oz) of the mushrooms into thin slices. Finely chop the lemongrass, ginger and 2 of the garlic cloves. Peel and finely dice the potato.

2. Heat ½ tablespoon of the vegetable oil in a medium saucepan. Once hot, add the spring onion whites to the pan and cook over a low-medium heat for 5 minutes until softened.

3. Crumble the 450g (1lb) remaining whole mushrooms into the pan with your hands and turn up the heat. Fry for 10 minutes until they have released all of their liquid and started to caramelize.

4. Add the chopped lemongrass, ginger and garlic, then cook for 2 minutes more. Add the potato, coconut milk and vegetable stock to the pan and bring the mixture to the boil. Turn the heat down and simmer for 15 minutes.

5. Transfer the mixture to a blender and blend until totally smooth, then pour back into the pan on the hob. Loosen with water if it's too thick, then season to taste with salt and pepper.

6. While your soup simmers, cook your toppings. Heat 1 tablespoon of vegetable oil in a frying pan and add the sliced mushrooms with a pinch of salt. Fry for 5 minutes over a high heat until they are caramelized and crispy. Drain on kitchen paper.

7. Thinly slice the remaining garlic clove.

8. Heat the remaining ½ tablespoon of vegetable oil in the same pan while you thinly slice the remaining garlic clove. Chuck the spring onion greens, chilli flakes and sliced garlic into the pan and fry for 2 minutes until crisp and sizzling.

9. Ladle the soup into bowls and top with the mushrooms and a spoonful of the flavoured oil. Serve up and enjoy.

Green
Udon

VG DF 30

There's something about the colour green that just screams freshness. When you eat this dish, you'll feel as amazing as it tastes – we've packed the green sauce with healthy fats and lots of micronutrients to make this a highly nutritious meal. Salted cashews are blended with coriander, ginger, lime and avocado to make the creamy, refreshing sauce.

Cook time: 30 mins

Ingredients

Serves 4

1 large ripe avocado
60g (2¼oz) roasted salted cashews
a small bunch of coriander
thumb-sized piece of fresh ginger
2 limes
4 spring onions
1 red chilli
200g (7oz) radishes
100g (3½oz) mangetout
2 × 300g (10½oz) packs of straight-to-wok udon noodles
200g (7oz) frozen peas
salt and black pepper

Method

1. Scoop the avocado into a blender, add the cashews, all the coriander stalks and most of the leaves. Finely grate in the ginger (no need to peel) and grate in the zest of both limes. Squeeze in the juice of 1 lime, add 175ml (6fl oz) of water and blitz to a smooth, vivid green sauce. Season to taste, adding the juice of the second lime if you think it needs it. Set aside.

2. Get your kettle on to boil while you thinly slice the spring onions (both green and white parts). Thinly slice the red chilli, seeds and all, radishes and mangetout. Scrape most of the veg into a large bowl, leaving a little behind to top the noodles.

3. Pour the boiled water into a large saucepan, bring back to the boil, then drop in the udon and peas. Cook for 1 minute, then drain both into a sieve and rinse briefly under cold water to cool. Shake off any excess water, then tip into the bowl of veg.

4. Pour in the dressing, give everything a toss to combine and coat the udon in the green sauce. Divide between four plates, scatter over the remaining veg and tear over the coriander leaves to serve. Enjoy.

Broccoli and *Pumpkin Seed* **Pesto Pasta**

30

We've taken a classic basil pesto and packed it with micronutrients – we've subbed in pumpkin seeds and anchovies for a source of healthy fat and protein and some broccoli for an added hit of veg. Then – because we're all about getting in as much flavour as possible – we've added garlic and chilli to the mix. An easy, low-effort dinner.

Cook time: 30 mins

Ingredients

Serves 4

100g (3½oz) pumpkin seeds
1 large broccoli head
100g (3½oz) spinach
50g (1¾oz) Parmesan, plus extra to serve
1 lemon
a small bunch of basil
3 tbsp olive oil, plus a drizzle to serve
300g (10½oz) pasta (we used casarecce)
3 fat garlic cloves
1 red chilli
50g (1¾oz) tin of anchovy fillets in oil
salt and black pepper

Method

1. Boil the kettle. Toast the pumpkin seeds in a dry frying pan over a medium heat until beginning to pop. Leave to cool. Cut the broccoli into smallish florets and roughly chop the stalk.

2. Pour the boiled water into a large saucepan, add salt and return to the boil. Drop in half the broccoli, cook for 5 minutes then tip in the spinach, stirring until just wilted. Using a slotted spoon, transfer both the broccoli and spinach to a sieve, leaving the pan of water over a low heat.

3. Tip the spinach and broccoli into a blender or food processor. Finely grate in the Parmesan and zest of the lemon. Add the basil, two-thirds of the toasted pumpkin seeds, the olive oil and 3 tablespoons of water. Blitz to a pesto, then season to taste with salt and pepper.

4. Bring the water back to the boil. Drop in the pasta and cook for 1 minute less than stated on the packet. Meanwhile, thinly slice the garlic and chilli, removing the seeds if you don't like things too hot.

5. Get a large high-sided frying pan over a medium–high heat. Tip in the anchovies, along with their oil, and smoosh with the back of your spoon until 'melted', then add the garlic and chilli. Cook for 1 minute, then tip in the remaining broccoli. Spoon in half a mugful of pasta water and cook for 3–4 minutes until the broccoli is just tender and coated in the sauce.

6. Drain the pasta, keeping back of another mugful of pasta water, then tip the pasta into the frying pan. Add the pesto and give everything a good mix to combine and warm through, stirring in enough pasta water to get to your desired consistency – we like it nice and saucy.

7. Season to taste with salt, pepper and lemon juice, scatter over the remaining pumpkin seeds, a grating of parmesan and drizzle with a little oil, to serve.

Smashed Peas on Toast *with Halloumi* **Croutons**

V 30

This is our new take on avo toast, blitzing up just-cooked peas – a more sustainable option with almost double the amount of protein – with mint, olive oil and lemon zest makes for a light, super-fresh pea smash that tastes great when topped with honey-coated halloumi croutons. Meet your new regular brunch.

Cook time: 25 mins

Ingredients

Serves 4

400g (14oz) frozen peas
a small bunch of mint leaves
1 tbsp olive oil, plus extra for drizzling (optional)
1 lemon
250g (9oz) pack of halloumi
2 tsp honey
1 tbsp sesame seeds
1–2 tsp chilli flakes (depending on how spicy you like it)
4 slices of bread (we like sourdough)
1 small garlic clove
salt and black pepper

Method

1. Cook the peas until just done, either in the microwave with a splash of water, or by pouring over boiling water in a bowl and leaving for a few minutes. Drain into a sieve. Tip into a food processor with half the mint leaves, the olive oil and zest of the lemon. Blitz to a kind of pea mash, adding a splash of water if it needs loosening. Season to taste.

2. Halloumi crouton time. Cut the halloumi into cubes while you get a large frying pan over a high heat. Add the halloumi and fry until deeply golden, about 2 minutes on each side, then drizzle over the honey, scatter over the sesame seeds and chilli flakes. Cook, tossing for 30 seconds more and remove from the heat.

3. While the halloumi is frying, toast the bread. Once toasted, cut the garlic in half and rub over the top of each piece, then drizzle each slice with a little olive oil, if using. Cut the lemon into four wedges.

4. Put one slice of toast on each plate. Top with the smashed peas and halloumi croutons, then tear over the remaining mint leaves and serve with the lemon wedges for squeezing over. Like avo toast, but better.

Tofu *Noodle* **Traybake**

VG DF 30

Picture a noodle stir-fry . . . but as a traybake. Tofu is a great protein source as it's low in saturated fat and rich in antioxidants, and this one-tray meal involves roasting your tofu and sprouts until they're crisp and then adding in noods and veggies with a deeply satisfying soy and black pepper sauce. A firm vegan favourite that you can get on the table in 30 minutes.

Cook time: 25 mins

Ingredients

Serves 4

460g (1lb) firm tofu (we like The Tofoo Co)
200g (7oz) Brussels sprouts
5 tbsp cornflour
2 tbsp rapeseed oil
1 tbsp black peppercorns
1 large red chilli
4 tsp maple syrup, plus a splash
3 tbsp rice wine vinegar
4 tbsp dark soy sauce
thumb-sized piece of fresh ginger
2 carrots
2 × 300g (10½oz) packs of straight-to-wok egg noodles
200g (7oz) sugar snap peas
salt and black pepper

Method

1. Preheat the oven to 220°C/200°C fan/gas mark 7.

2. Drain the tofu and cut it into medium cubes. Cut the sprouts in half. Spoon 4 tablespoons of the cornflour into a shallow bowl and season with salt and pepper. Toss the tofu in the cornflour mix so that it gets evenly coated.

3. Put the tofu onto one half of a large baking tray, leaving enough space between each cube so that they can crisp up. Spread the sprouts in an even layer onto the other half of the tray. Drizzle the oil evenly across the tofu and sprouts. Roast for 15–20 minutes until the sprouts are cooked through and charred and the tofu is crisp.

4. Meanwhile, toast the peppercorns in a dry frying pan over a medium heat until smelling great. Leave to cool slightly. Thinly slice the red chilli and add to a small bowl. Pour over a splash of maple syrup and 2 tablespoons of the rice wine vinegar, stir and leave to quick-pickle.

5. Crush the peppercorns then tip into a bowl. Add the remaining tablespoon of cornflour and 150ml (5fl oz) water and mix until the cornflour is fully combined before adding the remaining 4 teaspoons of maple syrup, 1 tablespoon of vinegar and the soy sauce. Set aside.

6. Next up, peel and cut the ginger and carrots into rough matchsticks then come back to your roasted tofu and sprouts. Add the noodles to the tin, breaking up any clumps with your spoon, then add the carrot, ginger, sugar snap peas and then finally the sauce. Give everything a good mix together and return to the oven for 5 minutes until the noodles and sugar snap peas are heated through and the sauce is reduced.

7. Divide between four bowls, top with the pickled red chilli and serve.

Ras El Hanout *Salmon with* **Bean Hummus**

GF DF 30

One for the cumin lovers out there, this speedy salmon is going to be a regular on your dinner table. We love the contrast between the fibre-filled silky tahini bean hummus and crunchy, spice-infused carrot salad.

Cook time: 30 mins

Ingredients

Serves 4

2 tbsp cumin seeds
2 × 400g (14oz) tins of butter beans
4 spring onions
a small bunch of coriander
4 medium carrots
60g (2¼oz) rocket
3 tbsp olive oil
2 lemons
4 skin-on salmon fillets
4 tsp ras el hanout
1 garlic clove
3 tbsp tahini
salt and black pepper
flatbreads, to serve (if you're extra hungry)

Gluten-Free: Serve with gluten-free flatbreads, if using.

Method

1. Preheat the oven to 200°C/180°C fan/gas mark 6 and line a baking tray with foil or baking paper.

2. Toast the cumin seeds in a dry frying pan over a medium heat until smelling amazing. Set aside to cool.

3. Salad time. Drain and rinse 1 tin of butter beans, then shake off any excess water and tip into your largest salad bowl.

4. Thinly slice the spring onions (both green and white parts) and roughly chop the coriander (stalks and all). Add these to the bowl. Peel and grate the carrots and add too, along with the rocket, three-quarters of the toasted cumin seeds and 2 tablespoons of the olive oil. Finely grate in the zest of both lemons. Toss together, then season to taste with salt, pepper and lemon juice. Set aside.

5. Next, lay the salmon fillets, skin-side down, on a cold frying pan and rub 1 teaspoon of ras el hanout over each one. Season with salt and pepper, drizzle with the remaining tablespoon of olive oil and fry for 7 minutes, then flip and cook for 2 more minutes until the salmon is just cooked and flakes easily.

6. Meanwhile, make the hummus. Drain the second tin of butter beans over a bowl, saving the liquid. Tip the beans into a food processor or blender and add the garlic, tahini, remaining cumin seeds and the juice of ½ lemon. Blitz until completely smooth, adding in some of the bean water until it's at your desired consistency – you'll need about half. Season to taste.

7. Scrape the hummus into a saucepan and place over a low heat, stirring occasionally to warm through.

8. Spread the warmed hummus onto four plates. Put a piece of salmon on top, drizzle over any oil from the pan, then pile the salad next to it. If you're really hungry, serve with flatbreads.

Tahini *Broth* **Noodles**

VG V DF 30

Tahini may sound a bit strange here, but it's actually the magic ingredient that turns this broth into a rich and creamy sauce, plus it adds protein and fat. Speedy and one-pan, this will become your go-to it's-a-weeknight-and-I-can't-be-bothered dinner. If cooking vegan, make sure to swap out the egg noodles for a vegan alternative.

Cook time: 20 mins

Ingredients

Serves 4

4 spring onions
thumb-sized piece of fresh ginger
3 fat garlic cloves
1 tbsp sesame seeds
2 tsp rapeseed oil
3 tbsp miso
1.4 litres (2½ pints) boiling vegetable stock
4 pak choi
1 red chilli
3 tbsp tahini
4 bunches of egg or medium noodles (approx. 200g/7oz)
4 handfuls of beansprouts
100g (3½oz) sugar snap peas

Make it Vegan: Use vegan noodles instead of egg noodles.

Method

1. Thinly slice the spring onions (both green and white parts), finely grate the ginger and garlic into a small bowl.

2. Toast the sesame seeds in a small dry frying pan over a medium heat until lightly golden. Set aside.

3. Get your largest saucepan over a medium–high heat. Pour in the rapeseed oil. Add most of the spring onions, cook until soft, then scrape in the grated ginger and garlic and cook, stirring, for 1 minute more. Add the miso, then pour in the vegetable stock. Give everything a good whisk so that the miso dissolves, then bring to a simmer.

4. Meanwhile, cut the pak choi in half and thinly slice the red chilli, seeds and all.

5. Come back to the broth. Whisk in the tahini – this will make it nice and creamy – then drop in the noodles and add the pak choi, standing them up with the leaves poking out of the water. Cook for 3 minutes. Stir through the beansprouts and sugar snaps, pushing the pak choi leaves into the broth. Cook for 2–3 minutes more until the noodles and pak choi are tender and everything is warmed through.

6. Divide the noodles and veg between four bowls, pour over the broth then top with the chilli, remaining spring onion and toasted sesame seeds to serve.

Curried Broccoli *with Turmeric* **Yoghurt**

V GF 30

This is one of those dishes that tastes and looks like you've made a massive effort, yet is actually super-simple to make. We've topped this fibre-packed dish with a zesty turmeric yoghurt and salty peanut and mustard seed dressing to give your gut a healthy boost and make the roasted broccoli really sing.

Cook time: 30 mins

Ingredients

Serves 4

2 large heads of broccoli
2 × 400g (14oz) tins of chickpeas
2 tbsp medium curry powder
3 tbsp rapeseed oil
thumb-sized piece of fresh ginger
1 lime
1 tsp ground turmeric
250g (9oz) natural yoghurt
1 banana shallot
2 fat garlic cloves
1 red chilli
50g (1¾oz) roasted salted peanuts
2 tsp mustard seeds
a handful of coriander leaves
salt and black pepper
garlic and coriander naan, to serve

Gluten-Free: Use gluten-free curry powder and swap naan for a gluten-free alternative.

Method

1. Preheat the oven to 220°C/200°C fan/gas mark 7.

2. Cut the broccoli into medium florets and roughly chop the stalks. Drain and rinse the chickpeas through a sieve, shaking off any excess water. Tip both into your largest roasting tin (or into two tins if that's easier), toss with the curry powder, 2 tablespoons of the rapeseed oil and plenty of seasoning. Spread into a single layer so that they cook evenly. Roast for 20–25 minutes until the broccoli is tender and a little charred and the chickpeas are crisp.

3. Meanwhile, finely grate the ginger (no need to peel) and lime zest into a bowl. Add the turmeric and yoghurt, stir together and season to taste. Set aside.

4. Dressing time. Thinly slice the shallot, garlic and chilli and roughly chop the peanuts. Get a small frying pan over a medium–high heat and pour in the remaining tablespoon of rapeseed oil. Add the shallot, fry until golden and then scrape in the garlic and chilli, cook for 1 minute more until the garlic is just golden. Add the peanuts and mustard seeds, as soon as the seeds start to pop and everything smells amazing, take the dressing off the heat and squeeze in the juice of the lime.

5. Spread the yoghurt across the base of a serving plate. Pile the broccoli and chickpeas on top, then spoon over the peanut dressing. Sprinkle with coriander leaves and serve with naan for scooping.

Sprout Salad *with Anchovy* **Dressing**

GF 30

This salad is a homage to the humble sprout – half are roasted and half are shredded and tossed with fresh apple, spicy caramelized nuts, pecorino and a dressing that's got strong Caesar vibes with healthy-fat anchovies to support the nervous system. The textures in this one are on point.

Cook time: 30 mins

Ingredients

Serves 4

100g (3½oz) unsalted mixed nuts
½ tsp chilli powder
2 tsp maple syrup
400g (14oz) Brussels sprouts
1 lemon
3 tbsp olive oil
50g (1¾oz) tin of anchovy fillets in oil
2 tsp Dijon mustard
1 small garlic clove
80g (2¾oz) pecorino
a small bunch of parsley
2 apples
salt and black pepper

Method

1. Preheat the oven to 180°C/160°C fan/gas mark 4 and line a baking tray with baking paper.

2. Toss the nuts onto the lined tray with the chilli powder and some seasoning. Toast in the oven for 6–8 minutes until lightly golden, then drizzle over the maple syrup. Return to the oven for 2 minutes until spicy and caramelized – yum. Leave to cool.

3. Meanwhile, very thinly slice half the Brussels sprouts (you can halve them and pulse in a food processor if easier). Tip the sliced sprouts into a serving bowl, season with salt and pepper, zest in all the lemon and squeeze in half the juice. Use your hands to massage the lemon juice into the sliced sprouts – this will help them soften.

4. Increase the oven temperature to 220°C/200°C fan/gas mark 7.

5. Cut the remaining sprouts in half. Tip onto a baking tray, drizzle with 1 tablespoon of the olive oil and season with salt and pepper. Arrange cut-side down in a single layer so that they cook evenly and roast for 15–20 minutes until cooked through and charred.

6. Dressing time. Put the anchovies along with their oil into a blender (or you can mash in a pestle and mortar if you prefer) along with the mustard, remaining 2 tablespoons of olive oil and remaining lemon juice. Finely grate in the garlic along with half the pecorino. Blitz until smooth, adding 2–3 tablespoons of water to loosen the dressing to a drizzle-able consistency. Season lightly – it will already be a flavour bomb.

7. Roughly chop the caramelized nuts and parsley (stalks and all). Core and thinly slice the apples. Shave the remaining pecorino.

8. Mix the charred sprouts, parsley, apple and most of the spiced nuts through the sliced sprouts. Drizzle over the anchovy dressing, then top with the remaining nuts and pecorino shavings to serve.

Cabbage *Aglio e* **Olio**

VG DF 30

Aglio e olio is up there in our top ten meals of all time because of how simple and satisfying it is. We've put a bit of a twist on it here by adding very thinly sliced hispi cabbage for an extra dose of veg and hit of vitamin C.

Cook time: 20 mins

Ingredients

Serves 4

320g ($11\frac{1}{4}$oz) linguine
8 garlic cloves
1 hispi cabbage (also known as sweetheart or pointed cabbage in the supermarket)
3 tbsp olive oil
$1\frac{1}{2}$–2 tsp chilli flakes (depending on how spicy you like it)
a small bunch of parsley
1 lemon
salt and black pepper

Method

1. Bring a large saucepan of salted water to the boil. Drop in the linguine and cook for 1 minute less than stated on the packet instructions.

2. Meanwhile, very thinly slice the garlic and cabbage, then get a large frying pan over a medium–high heat. Pour in the olive oil and add the garlic and chilli flakes. Cook, stirring, until the garlic turns lightly golden and is smelling amazing, then tip in the cabbage. Spoon in half a ladleful of pasta water, then simmer away for about 5 minutes until the cabbage has wilted and is tender.

3. Chop the parsley (stalks and all). Finely grate the lemon zest.

4. Using tongs, drain the linguine straight into the frying pan. Add the lemon zest and parsley and give everything a good toss to combine.

5. Season with salt, lots of black pepper and lemon juice to taste, then divide the pasta between four bowls. Simplicity at its best.

Sticky
Spicy
Turkey
Rice Bowls

This has midweek meal written all over it. Turkey mince is a lean source of protein and this recipe shows off what it can do when it's fried until crisp and caramelized, then coated in a sticky glaze of soy sauce, fish sauce and gochujang. Served with a fried egg, rice and kimchi, this dish delivers all the flavour in just 20 minutes.

Cook time: 20 mins

Ingredients

Serves 4

4 garlic cloves
3cm (1¼in) piece of fresh ginger
4 spring onions
1 tbsp gochujang
1 tbsp fish sauce
1 tbsp soy sauce
2 tbsp rapeseed oil
1 tsp chilli flakes
500g (1lb 2oz) turkey mince
2 pak choi
4 eggs
4 tbsp kimchi
rice, to serve

Gluten-Free: If you're cooking gluten-free, substitute the soy sauce for tamari.

Method

1. Grate the garlic and ginger. Finely chop the spring onions – reserve 1 tablespoon of the greens to garnish at the end.

2. Whisk together the gochujang, fish sauce and soy sauce.

3. Heat a tablespoon of the oil in a large wok and add the garlic, ginger, spring onions and chilli flakes. Fry over a high heat for 2 minutes until fragrant.

4. Add the turkey mince and fry for 10 minutes until crispy.

5. Meanwhile, put the pak choi into a bowl with a tablespoon of water. Cover with cling film and pop into the microwave for 2 minutes to steam it.

6. When the turkey is crispy, add the sauce and toss around for 1 minute until evenly coated.

7. Heat the remaining oil in a frying pan and fry up your eggs until crispy.

8. Serve the pork over rice, topped with the crispy fried eggs, kimchi and pak choi. Finish by scattering with the reserved spring onions.

Peanut *Chicken* **Curry**

GF DF 30

Midweek one-pan dinners that you can cook in half an hour are the stuff of dreams, and this is one of the dreamiest recipes. Yoghurt and peanut butter lend a creaminess to this curry without making it feel too heavy. We've amped up the protein using chicken and peanuts, making this a super-satisfying meal. We like serving it with rice, but roti would work nicely.

Cook time: 30 mins

Ingredients

Serves 4

4 banana shallots
5 garlic cloves
3cm (1¼in) piece of fresh ginger
4 skinless and boneless chicken breasts
2 tbsp coconut oil
a handful of fresh curry leaves
1 tbsp cumin seeds
1 tsp black mustard seeds
1 tsp chilli powder
½ tsp ground turmeric
a handful of coriander (stalks and all)
30g (1oz) salted peanuts
220g (7¾oz) spinach
150g (5½oz) natural or coconut yoghurt
5 tbsp peanut butter (smooth or crunchy)
salt

Method

1. Thinly slice the shallots and garlic and grate the ginger. Cut the chicken breasts into ½cm (¼in)-thin strips.

2. Get a large frying pan over a medium–high heat. Add 1 tablespoon of the coconut oil, then once melted, add half the chicken to the pan with a pinch of salt. Fry for a few minutes until it is browned on all sides, then use tongs to transfer to a bowl. Repeat with the remaining chicken.

3. Add the remaining tablespoon of coconut oil to the pan, then turn down the heat to low. Add the curry leaves, cumin seeds and black mustard seeds to the pan and cook for 1 minute until fragrant. The seeds will pop in the heat, so be careful.

4. Add the shallots to the pan, then cook for 5 minutes until completely softened. Add the chilli powder, turmeric, garlic and ginger and cook for 1 minute more. Return the chicken to the pan along with 500ml (17fl oz) of water, then bring the curry to a gentle simmer. Cook for 5 minutes over a medium–low heat.

5. Meanwhile, roughly chop the coriander and peanuts.

6. Once your 5 minutes are up, add the spinach to the curry and allow it to fully wilt. Stir in the yoghurt and peanut butter and season to taste with salt.

7. Sprinkle the curry with the coriander and peanuts and serve.

'Nduja & *Bean* **Soup**

30

Bean and veg-loaded broths are some of the simplest and heartiest midweek dinners you can make. Think of this a bit like a minestrone but with a whack of added heat from the 'nduja. We love the way ditalini looks here, but small macaroni would also work well. Experiment with whatever ingredients you've got to hand.

Cook time: 30 mins

Ingredients

Serves 4

1 onion
1 carrot
1 celery stick
2 tbsp olive oil
1 sprig of rosemary
60g (2¼oz) 'nduja
1 tsp tomato purée
200g (7oz) cherry tomatoes
1 litre (1¾ pints) chicken stock
1 × 400g (14oz) tin of cannellini beans
250g (9oz) ditalini or macaroni
200g (7oz) cavolo nero
20g (¾oz) Parmesan
salt and black pepper

Ingredient Hack: Save the cavolo nero stalks and freeze in an airtight container to use later in a stock.

Method

1. Very finely dice the onion, carrot and celery.

2. Heat the olive oil in a large saucepan. Add the diced veg and sprig of rosemary and cook over a medium heat for 15 minutes until softened, adding a splash of water if they start to stick.

3. Add the 'nduja to the pan along with the tomato purée. Cook, stirring, for 2 minutes until the 'nduja has released its oil and the mixture has darkened.

4. Halve the cherry tomatoes and add to the pan: cook for 5 minutes, squishing them up with the back of your spoon to break them down.

5. Add the chicken stock, then top it up with another 500ml (17fl oz) of water. Bring it to a simmer, then season to taste with salt.

6. Drain the cannellini beans, then tip these into the pan along with your pasta. Simmer for 5 minutes.

7. Meanwhile, tear the stalks away from the cavolo nero leaves and discard them. Tear the leaves into rough pieces. Once the 5 minutes are up, add the cavolo nero leaves to the pan. Simmer for another 3 minutes.

8. Check that your pasta is tender, then adjust the seasoning with salt and pepper. Spoon into bowls then grate over the Parmesan to serve. Enjoy!

Garlicky *Chicken & Egg* **Rice Bowls**

GF DF 30

Inspired by the beloved Japanese dish of oyakodon, this one-bowl meal gets its flavour from juicy chicken thighs and lots of garlic and spring onion. And when we say lots, we mean lots.

Cook time: 20 mins

Ingredients

Serves 4

1 onion
2 green chillies
10 garlic cloves
500g (1lb 2oz) skinless chicken thigh fillets
1 tbsp vegetable oil
200ml (7fl oz) chicken stock
3 tbsp soy sauce
3 tbsp Shaoxing wine
6 eggs
a bunch of spring onions
steamed short grain rice, to serve

Gluten-Free: If you're cooking gluten-free, substitute the soy sauce for tamari and check your stock is gluten-free.

Method

1. Thinly slice the onion, green chillies and garlic. Thinly slice the chicken thighs.

2. Heat the vegetable oil in a large frying pan, add the onion and green chillies and fry over a medium–high heat for about 5 minutes until softened but not coloured. Add in the garlic and cook for 1 minute more.

3. Add the sliced chicken, chicken stock, soy sauce and Shaoxing wine. Bring to a bubble and cook for 10 minutes over a medium–low heat.

4. Meanwhile, crack the eggs into a bowl and very gently mix a few times – you don't want the whites and eggs to be completely mixed. Thinly slice the spring onions (both green and white parts).

5. Pour the eggs over the chicken and gently swirl in with a wooden spoon and then sprinkle over three-quarters of the spring onions. Pop a lid on the pan and cook for 3 minutes until the eggs have set.

6. Spoon the chicken and eggs over bowls of steamed rice and then pour over any remaining liquid for the rice to absorb.

7. Sprinkle with the remaining spring onions and enjoy.

HEARTY

Roasted *Squash* **Dal**

VG GF DF

Sweet roasted squash is given the food processor treatment and then stirred through dal in this vegan comfort winner. On its own dal is a very wholesome meal, but we've upped the ante by adding butternut squash, and to cram in even more veg, we've made a tarka using tenderstem broccoli that tastes (and looks) unreal.

Cook time: 1 hr 15 mins

Ingredients

Serves 4

1 small butternut squash
3 tsp rapeseed oil
300g (10½oz) red split lentils
large thumb-sized piece of fresh ginger
3 fat garlic cloves
1 tsp ground turmeric
2 tsp ground cumin
200g (7oz) tenderstem broccoli
1 tbsp mustard seeds
1 tbsp cumin seeds
2 tsp coriander seeds
1 lime
1 green chilli
salt and black pepper
mango chutney and naan or rice, to serve

Method

1. Preheat the oven to 220°C/200°C fan/gas mark 7.

2. Quarter the butternut squash lengthways, remove the seeds then arrange in a roasting tin, cut-side down. Brush with 1 teaspoon of the oil and season with salt and pepper. Roast in the oven for 40–45 minutes until completely soft.

3. Once the squash has been roasting for 15 minutes, start the dal. Rinse the lentils in a sieve until the water runs clear, then tip into a large saucepan. Finely grate in the ginger and garlic and add the turmeric and some seasoning. Pour in 1.2 litres (2 pints) of water. Put over a high heat and bring to a simmer, then turn the heat down to medium and bubble away for 25–30 minutes until most of the liquid has been absorbed and the lentils are broken down and completely soft.

4. Come back to the squash. Scoop the flesh into a blender. Add the ground cumin and 100ml (3½fl oz) water. Blitz to a smooth sauce. Scrape the squash sauce into the cooked lentil dal, stir through and keep warm over a low heat.

5. Tarka time. Get a large frying pan over a high heat. Add the broccoli to the dry pan and cook for 4–5 minutes until beginning to char, then pour in 3 tablespoons of water. Continue to cook until all the water has evaporated and the broccoli is tender, then pour in the remaining 2 teaspoons of rapeseed oil. Add the mustard, cumin and coriander seeds and toss the broccoli with the seeds and the oil for a minute or so until smelling amazing. Remove from the heat.

6. Season the dal with salt, pepper and lime juice to taste. Thinly slice the green chilli, seeds and all.

7. Divide the dal between four bowls, top with the broccoli and all the whole spices, then scatter over the green chilli. Serve with mango chutney and naan or rice, if you like.

Caponata *Traybake* **Salad**

VG DF

Salads bulked out with charred seasonal veg and crispy croutons are the kinds of salads we want to eat. This sticky caponata number tossed in a sweet and sour dressing is a wonderful summer meal prep dish.

Cook time: 45 mins

Ingredients

Serves 4

3 thick slices of sourdough
2 aubergines
3 long peppers
2 red onions
a large handful of cherry tomatoes
4 tbsp olive oil
150g (5½oz) raisins
75g (2¾oz) capers
4 tbsp red wine vinegar
1 red chilli
1 garlic clove
a large handful of mint leaves
130g (4½oz) rocket
1 lemon
45g (1½oz) toasted pine nuts
salt and black pepper

Method

1. Preheat the oven to 220°C/200°C fan/gas mark 7.

2. Cut the sourdough into chunks and add to a large roasting tin.

3. Cut the aubergines and peppers into 2cm (¾in) chunks and the onions into wedges. Add to the roasting tin along with the whole cherry tomatoes.

4. Add 2 tablespoons of the olive oil to the veg and toss to coat. Season with salt and roast for 30 minutes until the bread is toasted and the veg is cooked through and starting to caramelize.

5. While the veg roasts, combine the raisins, capers and vinegar in a small bowl. Deseed and chop the chilli and add to the bowl.

6. Grate in the garlic clove and mix to combine. Chop the mint leaves, get them in the bowl and bring the whole lot together with the remaining 2 tablespoons of olive oil.

7. When the veg has roasted, allow to cool for 10 minutes, then stir through the dressing and the rocket. Season with salt and pepper, zest and squeeze over the lemon and top with the toasted pine nuts.

Corn
& Ricotta
Gnocchi

If you're debating what to have for dinner, make this. We used corn to make this sauce rich in fibre, which when combined with the ricotta creates a creamy sauce that wraps lovingly around the pillowy gnocchi, charred corn and loads of hot sauce. The epitome of a crowd-pleaser.

Cook time: 30 mins

Ingredients

Serves 4

4 fat garlic cloves
4 spring onions
4 corn on the cob
200ml (7fl oz) vegetable stock
150g (5½oz) ricotta
4 tbsp hot sauce (we like Frank's)
30g (1oz) butter
200g (7oz) spinach
500g (1lb 2oz) gnocchi
salt and black pepper
a big green salad, to serve

Method

1. Thinly slice the garlic cloves and spring onions (both green and white parts) while you boil a kettle.

2. Pour the boiling water into a saucepan and add salt. Once reboiling, drop in the corn cobs and cook for 3 minutes, then remove 2 of the cobs with tongs and transfer to a plate. Cook the remaining cobs for 3 minutes more until completely tender, then remove with tongs – making sure to keep the two lots of corn separate. Turn down the heat on the water to low.

3. Get a large frying pan searingly hot. Lay in the less-cooked corn and char the kernels, turning regularly. Once charred, set aside.

4. Holding the more-cooked corn upright, slice down with a knife, removing the kernels from the cob. Put these into a blender with the vegetable stock, ricotta and 2 tablespoons of hot sauce. Blitz to a velvety sauce and season to taste.

5. Come back to the charred corn. Cut the kernels off the cob and tip into a small bowl. Mix with the remaining 2 tablespoons of hot sauce and season.

6. Put the frying pan back over a medium heat. Melt in the butter, add the garlic and most of the spring onions and cook until soft, then tip the spinach into the pan.

7. At the same time turn the heat back up on the pan of water; once boiling, drop in the gnocchi and cook until the gnocchi just floats. Use a slotted spoon to add the cooked gnocchi to the frying pan with the spinach.

8. Pour in the sweetcorn sauce, toss everything together to warm through and season to taste. Divide between four bowls, top with the charred hot sauce corn and remaining spring onions. Serve with a big green salad on the side. Get in.

Charred Aubergine **Dhansak**

VG GF DF

Dhansak is a popular Indian curry usually made with goat or mutton. We've created an untraditional vegan riff on it, using aubergine instead. We also used coconut oil here as it is better when heated at high temperatures. Herby coconut yoghurt really livens up this fuss-free recipe.

Cook time: 1 hr 5 mins

Ingredients

Serves 4

2 aubergines
1 onion
thumb-sized piece of fresh ginger
4 fat garlic cloves
1 tbsp coconut oil
1–2 tsp chilli powder (depending on how spicy you like it)
2 tsp ground coriander
1 tsp ground turmeric
2 tsp fenugreek seeds (or cumin seeds)
1 × 400g (14oz) tin of plum tomatoes
100g (3½oz) red split lentils
a bunch each of coriander and mint
300g (10½oz) coconut yoghurt
3 tsp garam masala
1 lemon
salt and black pepper
rice or naan, to serve

Gluten-Free: Serve with rice or a gluten-free naan alternative.

Method

1. Cut the aubergines into roughly 3cm (1in) cubes while you get a large, high-sided frying pan over a high heat. Add half the aubergine to the pan and dry-fry for about 4 minutes, turning halfway, until the aubergine is beginning to collapse and is a little charred. Tip into a bowl and repeat with the remaining aubergine.

2. Finely chop the onion, ginger and garlic. Put the pan back over a medium heat, melt in the coconut oil and add the onion. Cook, stirring occasionally, until soft, then add the ginger and garlic and cook for 1 minute more.

3. Spoon in the chilli powder, ground coriander, turmeric and fenugreek or cumin seeds.

4. Give everything a good stir until smelling amazing, then tip in the plum tomatoes, along with 1½ tins of water. Stir in the lentils, bring the curry to a simmer and cook for 15 minutes. Add the aubergine to the curry, cover and cook for 15–20 minutes more until the aubergine and lentils are cooked through.

5. Herby yoghurt time. Put most of the coriander (stalks and all) and mint leaves into a blender or food processor along with the coconut yoghurt and 1 teaspoon of the garam masala. Blitz until smooth-ish, season to taste with salt, pepper and lemon juice.

6. Come back to the curry: stir though the remaining 2 teaspoons of garam masala and season to taste – you may want to add some of the remaining lemon juice here.

7. Spoon the yoghurt over the curry and tear over the remaining herbs. Serve with rice or naan – your choice.

Garlicky Loaded *Potato* **Skins**

V **GF**

We've packed garlicky potato skins with a healthy dose of green veg and draped over a tangy cornichon-spiked salsa verde. Need we say more? This is comforting to the core.

Cook time: 1 hr 30 mins

Ingredients

Serves 4

4 medium baking potatoes
1 garlic bulb
2 leeks
200g (7oz) cavolo nero
3 tbsp olive oil
200g (7oz) frozen peas
3 tsp Dijon mustard
80g (2¾oz) Comté or Gruyère
8 cornichons
a small handful of parsley
2 tbsp red wine vinegar
salt and black pepper
big green salad, to serve (optional)

Ingredient Hack: If you can't find cavolo nero, use regular kale instead.

Method

1. Preheat the oven to 200°C/180°C fan/gas mark 6.

2. Prick the potatoes all over with a sharp knife. Wrap the whole garlic bulb in foil. Put the potatoes into a roasting tin, season and bake for 1 hour until completely tender, adding the wrapped garlic to the tin after 20 minutes. After 40 minutes it should be super soft.

3. Meanwhile, halve and thinly slice the leeks. Using one hand, hold each cavolo nero stalk and use the other to strip the leaves away from the stalk, then finely chop the stalks.

4. Get a large frying pan over a medium heat. Add 2 teaspoons of the olive oil, the sliced leeks and chopped cavolo nero stalks along with 3 tablespoons of water. Cook until the water has evaporated and the leeks are collapsed and soft. Add the cavolo nero leaves and peas and cook for a few minutes more until everything is tender. Stir through 2 teaspoons of the mustard, then scrape into a large bowl and set aside.

5. Once the garlic is cooked, squeeze out onto a chopping board, mash with a fork then stir through the greens.

6. Cut the baked potatoes in half and leave to cool a little, then spoon the potato centre into the greens and mix together. Increase the oven temperature to 220°C/200°C fan/gas mark 7.

7. Put the potato skins back into the roasting tin, drizzle with the remaining teaspoon of olive oil and bake for 5 minutes so that they crisp up slightly.

8. Meanwhile, grate the cheese. Season the filling to taste and then load into the potato skins and sprinkle over the cheese. Return to the oven for 10 minutes until bubbling and golden.

9. Salsa verde time. Chop the cornichons and parsley (stalks and all) and mix together with the remaining teaspoon of mustard, 2 tablespoons of olive oil and the red wine vinegar. Season to taste – you want it punchy. Serve the cornichon salsa verde with the loaded potato skins and a big green salad, if you like.

Baked Rice *with Pomegranate* & Pistachio

VG V GF DF

Everyone loves a recipe they can whack in the oven and forget about. This is one of those. The rice and veg bake at the same time, in their own spiced stock and the end result is pretty magic. We love the addition of orange in this baked rice – along with pistachios and pomegranate seeds this recipe is packed with micronutrients.

Cook time: 1 hr

Ingredients

Serves 4

250g (9oz) basmati rice
1 large aubergine
1 cauliflower
1 large red onion
3 garlic cloves
1 orange
2 tbsp ras el hanout
2 tbsp harissa (we like rose harissa)
750ml (1¼ pints) boiling vegetable stock
2 tbsp olive oil
50g (1¾oz) pistachios
a large handful of mint
4 tbsp pomegranate seeds
salt and black pepper
yoghurt, to serve (optional)

Make it Vegan/Dairy-Free: Serve with dairy-free yoghurt.

Budget Hack: Swap out the pistachios for toasted pumpkin seeds instead.

Gluten-Free: Use gluten-free stock.

Method

1. Preheat the oven to 200°C/180°C fan/gas mark 6.

2. Rinse the rice through a sieve until the water is no longer cloudy. Shake off the excess water, then tip the rice into a deep medium roasting dish.

3. Cut the aubergine into cubes and the cauliflower into small florets around the same size. Roughly chop the cauliflower stalk and leaves too, then chop the red onion. Add everything to the rice.

4. Finely grate the garlic into the rice, followed by the orange zest, then squeeze in the orange juice. Spoon in the ras el hanout and harissa. Pour in the vegetable stock, season generously with salt and pepper, then give a good mix and spread out into an even layer.

5. Drizzle over the olive oil. Roast in the oven, uncovered, for 40 minutes until everything is cooked and the stock has absorbed.

6. Meanwhile, toast the pistachios in a dry frying pan over a medium heat until just beginning to darken. Leave to cool, then roughly chop. Pick the mint leaves and stir through the pistachios along with the pomegranate seeds and a little salt.

7. Once the rice is baked, spoon over the pistachio and pomegranate topping and serve in the dish for people to help themselves, with some yoghurt if you like.

Meatball *Macaroni Soup* **with Salsa Verde**

Meatballs and pasta is an Italian classic, as is minestrone. Put the two together and what have you got? Something that's not very classic, admittedly, but something that tastes very good indeed. We've reduced the amount of macaroni to keep this dish balanced – perfect as an everyday meal.

Cook time: 1 hr 10 mins

Ingredients

Serves 4

500g (1lb 2oz) beef mince
1 large onion
5 garlic cloves
3 tsp dried oregano
100g (3½oz) fresh breadcrumbs
1 egg
2 carrots
2 celery sticks
4 tbsp olive oil
50g (1¾oz) Parmesan, plus the rind
2 tsp chilli flakes
1 × 400g (14oz) tin of plum tomatoes
1.2 litres (2 pints) chicken stock
100g (3½oz) macaroni
100g (3½oz) spinach
a bunch of parsley
2 tsp capers
1 lemon
salt and black pepper

Method

1. Tip the beef mince into a large bowl. Coarsely grate in half the onion and 2 of the garlic cloves. Add 1 teaspoon of the oregano, the breadcrumbs and plenty of seasoning, then crack in the egg. Using your hands, scrunch the flavourings through the meat, then shape into 20 small meatballs. Put into a roasting tin and slide into the fridge to chill while you start the soup.

2. Finely chop the remaining onion half and the carrots and celery. Get your largest saucepan over a medium heat. Pour in 2 tablespoons of the olive oil, then tip in the veg along with a pinch of salt and cook, stirring occasionally, until soft.

3. Meanwhile finely chop the remaining 3 garlic cloves and cut the rind off the Parmesan. Add the garlic, the remaining 2 teaspoons of dried oregano and the chilli flakes to the pan and cook for a minute more. Tip in the plum tomatoes, add the Parmesan rind and pour in the stock. Bring the soup to the boil, breaking down the tomatoes with the back of your spoon, then bubble for 10 minutes.

4. Preheat the oven to 200°C/180°C fan/gas mark 6.

5. Brush the meatballs with 1 tablespoon of olive oil. Bake in the oven for 12–15 minutes until cooked and browned.

6. Meanwhile drop the macaroni into the soup and cook for 1 minute less than stated on the packet instructions. Once cooked, stir in the spinach until wilted, then season the soup to taste.

7. While your pasta cooks, make the salsa verde. Roughly chop the parsley (stalks and all) and add to a mini food processor along with the capers, the juice of the lemon and the remaining tablespoon of olive oil. Add a tablespoon of water and whizz to a rough sauce, then season to taste with salt.

8. Divide the soup between four bowls and top each with five meatballs. Add a spoonful of salsa verde to each one and finely grate over the Parmesan to serve.

Misha's *Salt-Baked* **Sea Bass**

DF

One for a special occasion. Perfectly tender, flaky fish with delicious caramelised potatoes and garlicky kale. A Valentine's Day classic.

Make sure you tell the Mob to watch out for bones.

Cook time: 1 hour

Ingredients

Serves 4

300g (10½oz) new potatoes
100g (3½oz) cherry tomatoes
olive oil
a bunch of thyme
1 whole sea bass (about 1.75kg/3lb 12oz), gutted and scaled
1 lemon
2–3kg (4lb 8oz–6lb 10oz) coarse sea salt
200g (7oz) cavolo nero
1 tsp chilli flakes
salt and black pepper

For the chilli oil
1 red chilli
5 tbsp extra virgin olive oil
1 lemon

Method

1. Preheat the oven to 200°C/180°C fan/gas mark 6.

2. Cut the new potatoes and tomatoes roughly into halves, then spread out in one layer in a roasting tin.

3. Pour over a good few glugs of olive oil, then scatter over 2–3 sprigs of thyme, a couple of pinches of salt and a good grind of pepper. Toss together, then put onto the top shelf of the oven. After 20 minutes, give everything a good shake and bakr for another 15 minutes.

4. Meanwhile, prep your fish. Pat the sea bass dry with some kitchen paper and rub a pinch of salt into the cavity. Cut 3–4 lemon slices and stuff into the cavity with a few thyme sprigs. Pour the coarse sea salt into a large bowl, add 4 tablespoons of water and stir together. Tip a layer of salt about 1cm (½in) thick into a roasting tin large enough to hold the fish, just under where the fish will sit and place the fish on top. Then cover the whole fish with the rest of the salt, patting down until you have encased the entire thing neatly in a salt mound.

5. Back to the potatoes. Once all the liquid from the tomatoes has evaporated and everything is becoming golden and sticky. Slide the fish onto the shelf below the potatoes and cook for 25 minutes.

6. Meanwhile, strip the cavolo nero leaves from the tough stems and chop them into strips about 4cm (1½in) thick. Steam these for 3 minutes, then tip into a bowl. Add a squeeze of lemon juice, the chilli flakes, a good glug of olive oil and a pinch of salt and pepper and give it a good mix.

7. Take out the fish and check to see if the potatoes are done. The tomatoes should have disintegrated and everything should be golden and sticky. If they aren't ready yet, whack the oven temperature up to 220°C/200°C fan/gas mark 7 for 5–10 minutes.

8. Make the chilli oil: finely chop the chilli and whisk into the olive oil along with grated zest and juice of the lemon.

9. When everything is ready, smash the top of the salt crust with the back of a spoon and clear away all the salt. Peel off the skin and use a large knife or fish slice to serve the fish.

10. Once the top side of the fish is served, peel back and remove the fish bones to get at the fillet underneath. Serve the fish drizzled with the chilli oil, with the potatoes and tomatoes and cavolo nero alongside.

Roasted Cauliflower *Mac* **& Cheese**

V

It's a cold winter's night, you've been caught in the rain, and really fancy a comforting cheesy meal. The only catch is that you also want to get in your five-a-day. Here's your dish. Blitzed-up roasted cauliflower, a good source of fibre, B6 and potassium, creates an unctuous pasta sauce while a healthy dose of Parmesan will satisfy your cheese cravings.

Cook time: 1 hr 15 mins

Ingredients

Serves 4

1 large cauliflower
1 garlic bulb
1 tbsp olive oil
50g (1¾oz) butter
4 tbsp capers
300g (10½oz) macaroni
75g (2¾oz) Parmesan (or vegetarian alternative)
a handful of parsley
20g (¾oz) panko breadcrumbs
100g (3½oz) ball of mozzarella
salt and black pepper

Method

1. Preheat the oven to 200°C/180°C fan/gas mark 6.

2. Cut the cauliflower up into medium-sized florets, including the stalks and leaves. Place the stalks and florets onto a baking tray along with the whole garlic bulb and drizzle with the olive oil. Season with salt and pepper and roast for 30 minutes, then add the cauliflower leaves to the tray, toss to combine and return to the oven to roast for another 15 minutes.

3. Meanwhile, get a large saucepan of water on to boil.

4. Add the butter to a frying pan. Once melted, add the capers and fry until crispy. Your butter will brown in this time – watch for the little flecks of white turning golden. Take the pan off the heat, then remove your capers with a slotted spoon and set aside.

5. Add ¾ of the cauliflower florets, along with all of the stalks, to a blender. Squeeze the cooked garlic cloves out of their skins into the blender, then pour in the brown butter and 200ml (7fl oz) of water and blend to a sauce.

6. Add salt to the saucepan of boiling water, then add your macaroni. Cook until al dente, then drain, reserving a couple of mugs of pasta water.

7. Preheat the grill to medium–high.

8. Finely grate the Parmesan and set aside about a tablespoon for the topping. Pour the cauliflower sauce into a large frying pan, add the grated cheese and stir to melt in. Add a little pasta water to loosen, then tip in the pasta and remaining cauliflower. Mix to combine, adding more pasta water if necessary.

9. Finely chop the parsley (stalks and all). Add to a bowl with the panko breadcrumbs and remaining grated Parmesan and mix.

10. Pour the cauliflower cheese into a baking dish and top with the reserved crispy capers. Tear over the mozzarella and scatter with the parsley breadcrumbs. Grill for 5–10 minutes until bubbling and golden. Enjoy.

moh

Cavolo Nero *& Wild Mushroom* **Risotto**

V **GF**

This is perfect for a special occasion dinner when you're willing to dedicate your time to creating something truly delicious. We've added some extra greens to this risotto by throwing in cavolo nero – high in fibre and calcium – and finished it with garlicky mushrooms and Parmesan cream. What more could you ask for?

Cook time: 40 mins

Ingredients

Serves 4

25g (1oz) butter
1 onion
4 garlic cloves
200g (7oz) cavolo nero
250g (9oz) arborio rice
200ml (7fl oz) white wine
1.5 litres (2½ pints) vegetable stock
80g (2¾oz) Parmesan (or vegetarian alternative)
500g (1lb 2oz) mixed mushrooms
1 tbsp olive oil
a handful of parsley
1 lemon
100ml (3½fl oz) single cream
salt and black pepper

Ingredient Hack: Save the cavolo nero stalks and put into an airtight container, then freeze to use later in a stock.

Gluten-Free: Use gluten-free stock.

Method

1. Melt the butter in a large high-sided frying pan over a low-medium heat. Finely dice and add the onion and cook for about 10 minutes until soft but not brown. Thinly slice and add 2 of the garlic cloves and cook for another 2 minutes.

2. Bring a saucepan of salted water to the boil. Strip the cavolo nero from its stalks, roughly chop the leaves and boil for 5 minutes. Drain and blitz in a blender until smooth, adding water to blend.

3. Once the onions are cooked, add the rice and cook for about a minute, stirring, until the rice is turning translucent at the edges.

4. Pour in the wine, turn the heat up to medium and let it bubble away until almost completely evaporated.

5. Now begin adding stock, a ladleful at a time, stirring as you go and only adding more stock once each ladle has been absorbed. Once all of the stock has been absorbed, the rice should be rich and creamy and almost cooked through but still with a little bite.

6. Spoon in the cavolo nero purée and finely grate in half the Parmesan. Cook for another minute, then turn the heat to super low, cover and keep warm while you cook the mushrooms.

7. Thinly slice the mushrooms, then heat the olive oil in a large pan over a high heat. Add the mushrooms and fry with a pinch of salt until browned.

8. Once the mushrooms have some colour, finely chop the remaining 2 garlic cloves and parsley (stalks and all). Add to the mushroom pan and cook for another minute or so. Turn off the heat, squeeze in the juice of the lemon and toss.

9. Warm the cream in a small pan but turn off the heat when it starts to steam. Grate in the remaining Parmesan, grind in about a teaspoon of black pepper and stir until the Parmesan has melted and the mix is thick and creamy.

10. Plate up the risotto and top with the garlicky mushrooms and a drizzle of the Parmesan cream.

The Freshest **Ribollita**

VG DF

This rustic Tuscan stew is a real winter warmer. Not only is it a deliciously cost-effective way of using up leftover bread and vegetables, but it's also completely vegan. Here we've upped the amount of beans for a boost of protein and fibre.

Cook time: 1 hr 15 mins

Ingredients

Serves 4

2 tbsp olive oil, plus a drizzle to serve
1 onion
1 carrot
1 celery stick
2 bay leaves
1 rosemary sprig
½ tsp chilli flakes
3 garlic cloves
1 × 400g (14oz) tin of plum tomatoes
1 litre (1¾ pints) vegetable stock
2 × 400g (14oz) tins of cannellini beans
150g (5½oz) cavolo nero
4 slices of ciabatta
30g (1oz) grated Parmesan (optional)
salt and black pepper

Ingredient Hacks: Feel free to add or swap the veggies around. Kale, parsnips, fennel or cabbage are all nice options. Save the cavolo nero stalks and put into an airtight container in the freezer to use in a stock.

Make it Vegan/Dairy-Free: By leaving out the cheese.

Method

1. Warm the olive oil in a large heavy-based pan over a medium heat. Dice the onion, carrot and celery and add to the pan with a pinch of salt.

2. Sweat the mix down for a few minutes, then add the bay leaves, rosemary, chilli flakes and 2 of the whole garlic cloves.

3. Cook for another few minutes until fragrant. Break up the plum tomatoes into a bowl, then add to the pan with the vegetable stock.

4. Drain one of the tins of beans through a sieve, tip into a bowl then use a fork to mash them up into a paste. Add to the pan and mix well until it becomes slightly thick. Cook for about 30 minutes.

5. While the ribollita cooks, strip the cavolo nero leaves firmly from the stalks and roughly chop them. Add the cavolo nero leaves and your second tin of beans, along with their liquid, to the pan and cook for a further 20 minutes.

6. Meanwhile, toast the ciabatta then rub the toast with the remaining cut garlic clove.

7. Once the ribollita is ready, season with salt and pepper to taste.

8. Now the important bit – place a slice of the garlicky toast into the bottom of each bowl and pour the stew on top. Leave it for a few minutes until the bread goes soft (trust us). Add a drizzle of olive oil and a sprinkle of cheese, if you like. Enjoy.

Spicy Cauliflower *& Tahini* **Soup**

VG GF DF

A spiced tahini and roasted cauliflower soup filled with plenty of lovely caramelized veg. The crunchy fried parsley garnish is a game-changer and the tahini rounds this dish off nicely with a good source of healthy fats.

Cook time: 1 hr 15 mins

Ingredients

Serves 4

1 large cauliflower
3 small potatoes
2 garlic bulbs
3 tbsp olive oil
3 tsp ground cumin
3 tsp sumac
3 tsp smoked paprika
1 onion
2 litres (3½ pints) vegetable stock
3 tbsp tahini, plus a drizzle to serve
3 red chillies
a small handful of parsley
1 tsp cumin seeds
1 tbsp sesame seeds
salt and black pepper

Gluten-Free: Use gluten-free stock.

Method

1. Preheat the oven to 180°C/160°C fan/gas mark 4.

2. Roughly chop the cauliflower into small pieces, including the stems and leaves, before dicing the potatoes into equally small pieces, leaving the skin on. Next, slice one of the garlic bulbs in half horizontally. (Separate the other bulb into cloves for later.)

3. Tip the potato and cauliflower pieces into a large roasting tin along with the halved garlic bulb and pour over 2 tablespoons of the olive oil. Sprinkle with 2 teaspoons of the ground cumin, 2 teaspoons of the sumac, 2 teaspoons of the smoked paprika, and 1 teaspoon salt. Massage it all well into the veg with your hands and pop into the oven for 40 minutes until the cauliflower is crispy and the potato cooked through. (You may need to use two roasting tins.)

4. Pick out a handful of the prettiest cauliflower florets and crispiest potato cubes and save these to garnish.

5. Dice the onion and roughly chop 3 garlic cloves. Heat ½ tablespoon of the oil in your largest saucepan and sauté the onion and garlic over a medium–high heat for 5 minutes until the onion turns translucent. Add the remaining smoked paprika and ground cumin and toast for 30 seconds.

6. Now add the roasted veg. Tip the crispy potatoes and cauliflower into the pan, squeezing out the soft flesh of the garlic cloves, then pour in the stock. Simmer and then blend with a stick blender until smooth. Add the tahini and season with salt. Adjust the thickness with water to the consistency of double cream.

7. Thinly slice the remaining garlic, the chillies and parsley. Pour the remaining ½ tablespoon of olive oil into a small frying pan and place over a medium–high heat. Fry the cumin seeds for 1 minute until they start to pop. Add the sliced garlic and chillies and the sesame seeds and fry for 2 minutes until the garlic is lightly golden. Add the sliced parsley and cook for 30 seconds until the parsley is crispy. Season with salt and pepper.

8. Ladle the soup into bowls and top with the crispy garlic, chilli and parsley. Finally, layer on the reserved roasted cauliflower florets and crispy potatoes and top with a drizzle of tahini and sprinkle with the remaining teaspoon of sumac. Enjoy hot.

Charred Hispi with *Herby* **Yoghurt**

V GF 30

This is our contribution to the charred cabbage trend, tossing it in a spicy honey vinegar dressing and laying it on a bed of cooling herby yoghurt. The combination of cabbage, vinegar and yoghurt means this is packed with gut-friendly nutrients to aid digestion and replenish your gut microbiome. Meet your new favourite side.

Cook time: 25 mins

Ingredients

Serves 4

1 large hispi cabbage
1 tbsp olive oil
2 tbsp honey
2 tbsp white wine vinegar
1 lime
1 red chilli
1 green chilli
a handful of coriander
a handful of mint
300g (10½oz) Greek yoghurt
salt and black pepper

Ingredient Hack: Hispi is a delicious cabbage variety that is slightly sweeter than regular green cabbage. You might also see them called sweetheart cabbage.

Method

1. Start by removing the outer leaves of the cabbage and giving it a rinse, then cut into quarters.

2. Heat a large frying pan over a medium heat and add the olive oil. Add the cabbages to the pan with the outer side down and cook for about 5 minutes, moving around a little as they cook.

3. Season the cabbages all over with salt and pepper, then flip onto the cut side. You'll want to cook each cut side for about 3 or 4 minutes until they have a lovely golden brown colour.

4. While the cabbages cook, mix the honey, white wine vinegar and zest and juice of the lime in a small bowl.

5. Finely chop both chillies and all of the herbs. Mix the chillies into the honey vinegar and the herbs into the yoghurt.

6. Once the cabbage is cooked, remove from the pan and, while still warm, drizzle all over with the honey vinegar.

7. Spread 2 tablespoons of yoghurt onto each plate, top with a wedge of the hispi cabbage and enjoy.

FRESHEST

Chargrilled Courgette *& Butter Bean* **Salad**

VG **DF**

Creamy butter beans and caramelized courgettes are tossed in a fresh lemon and herb dressing for this beauty of a late summer salad. As always, we've thought about texture by adding some toasted flaked almonds for a satisfying crunch. The wonderful variety of vitamins from the herbs and lemon juice are absorbed easily thanks to the healthy fats in the almonds and olive oil.

Cook time: 40 mins

Ingredients

Serves 4

200g (7oz) orzo
4 courgettes
2 lemons
4 tbsp olive oil
a bunch of mint
a bunch of parsley
1 green chilli
1 tsp Dijon mustard
30g (1oz) flaked almonds
1 red chilli
1 × 400g (14oz) tin of butter beans
salt and black pepper

Fresh Hack: This nutritious salad provides a wonderful variety of vitamins from the herbs and lemon juice, which are absorbed more easily thanks to healthy fats from the almonds and olive oil.

Method

1. Get a big saucepan of water on to boil. Add some salt, then tip in the orzo and cook for 6 minutes. Drain and leave to cool.

2. Meanwhile, slice the courgettes into 1cm (½in)-thick slices on a slight diagonal. Pop them in a bowl, then squeeze over the juice of half a lemon. Drizzle with 2 tablespoons of the olive oil and scatter over a good pinch of salt, then toss in the bowl so that the courgettes are totally coated.

3. Heat a griddle pan over a medium–high heat and add the courgettes a few at a time. Fry for a few minutes on each side until they're golden and starting to char. Remove from the pan and repeat with the remaining courgettes.

4. While your courgettes fry, make the herby dressing. Roughly chop the mint, parsley and green chilli and add to a food processor along with the juice of the remaining lemons and a big pinch of salt. Add the Dijon mustard, the remaining 2 tablespoons of olive oil and a splash of water, then blend to a sauce. Adjust the seasoning if needed.

5. Toast the flaked almonds in the dry frying pan for a few minutes until golden. Thinly slice the red chilli.

6. Drain the butter beans, then toss the courgettes, butter beans and orzo in the herby dressing before serving sprinkled with the almonds and sliced red chilli.

Chicken Meatballs *with Sesame* **Greens**

GF DF

This is a hybrid of two Japanese dishes: *tsukune* and *goma-ae*. The chicken meatballs (low in saturated fat – a great alternative to beef) couldn't be simpler; you'll be making the sticky glaze on repeat. The tahini-dressed spinach salad, on the other hand, is a lesson on how to utilize fresh flavours without any unnecessary frills.

Cook time: 1 hr

Ingredients

Serves 4

You will need 8 small skewers, soaked in cold water (or try our hack) and ice

2 tbsp mirin, plus 4 tsp
2 tbsp dark soy sauce, plus 2 tsp
2 tsp honey
4 spring onions thumb-sized piece of fresh ginger
500g (1lb 2oz) chicken mince
1½ tbsp cornflour
400g (14oz) spinach
400g (14oz) fine green beans
4 tbsp tahini
2 tbsp sesame seeds
1 tsp rapeseed oil
salt and black pepper
rice, to serve

Gluten-Free: If cooking gluten-free use tamari instead of soy sauce.

Cooking Hack: If you don't have skewers, shape the chicken into small hamburger-shaped patties instead and cook in exactly the same way.

Method

1. Mix the 2 tablespoons of mirin, 2 tablespoons of soy sauce, honey and 4 tablespoons of water together in a small bowl. Set aside (this is your meatball glaze).

2. Thinly slice the spring onions (both green and white parts). Scrape most of them into a large bowl, finely grate in the ginger, then tip in the chicken mince. Add the cornflour along with plenty of seasoning, then beat the mixture together with a wooden spoon for a couple of minutes until sticky. Using wet hands, create 24 small meatballs, threading three onto each skewer. Put onto a baking tray and into the fridge.

3. Get your largest saucepan of salted water on to boil. Next to it fill a large bowl with ice-cold water. Once the water is boiling, drop in the spinach. Cook until just wilted, then using a slotted spoon drain into the bowl of cold water. Once cold, pick out the spinach with your hands, keeping the bowl of cold water, and squeeze as much water out of the spinach as possible. Put into a large bowl.

4. Add the green beans to the pan of boiling water and cook for about 2 minutes until just tender; again drain into the cold water. Once cool, drain, shake off any excess water and add to the spinach.

5. Dressing time. Mix the tahini, 4 teaspoons of mirin and 2 teaspoons of soy sauce together in a bowl and add water to make it a thick drizzle-able consistency (about 3 tablespoons). Set aside.

6. Toast the sesame seeds in a dry frying pan over a medium heat until lightly golden and leave to cool.

7. Get your largest non-stick frying pan or griddle pan searingly hot. Drizzle with the oil, spreading it across the base, then lay in the chicken skewers. Cook for 3–4 minutes on each side until cooked through and caramelized, then pour in the glaze and cook over a low heat, turning regularly, for a couple of minutes until sticky.

8. Add the dressing and sesame seeds over the greens and toss.

9. Serve the greens on top of the rice, alongside the meatballs, scattering over the remaining spring onions to serve.

Loaded Turkey *Burritos with* **Pineapple Salsa**

We've used turkey mince for these burritos, which is low in saturated fat but high in protein. One of our recipe testers fed this to her friend, who they said they'd buy the book based on this recipe alone. Not really anything more to be said.

Cook time: 35 mins

Ingredients

Serves 4

1 red onion
½ small pineapple
a small bunch of coriander
2 limes
2 tbsp hot sauce (we like sriracha)
150g (5½ oz) natural yoghurt
½ small red cabbage
1 tbsp olive oil
500g (1lb 2oz) turkey mince
3 tbsp fajita seasoning
250g (9oz) cooked long grain rice
2 avocados
4 large tortilla wraps
salt and black pepper
a handful of pickled jalapeños, to serve (optional)

Ingredient Hack: Make your own fajita seasoning by mixing 2 teaspoons of chilli powder, 2 teaspoons of ground cumin, 1 teaspoon of garlic powder, 1 teaspoon of ground oregano and 1 teaspoon of smoked paprika together in a small bowl.

Cooking Hack: This one makes a lot of filling, so if you can only find the smaller wraps, double up on your burritos.

Method

1. Start with the salsa. Very finely chop the red onion. Scrape half into a small bowl. Peel and dice the pineapple and add to the bowl of onion. Roughly chop half the coriander (stalks and all) and add this too. Zest and squeeze in the juice of 1 lime, season and set the salsa aside.

2. Next, stir the hot sauce into the yoghurt and season. Very finely shred the cabbage and scrape into a new bowl. Squeeze over the juice of the other lime, season then scrunch together with your hands – this will help it soften slightly.

3. Get a large frying pan over a high heat. Pour in the olive oil, then tip in the turkey mince. Use the back of your spoon to break the mince into smaller pieces, season, then add the remaining chopped red onion. Fry, stirring occasionally, until the mince is cooked through and browned, then stir through the fajita seasoning.

4. Meanwhile, heat the rice until piping hot, roughly chop the remaining coriander and mix together. Slice the avocados.

5. Assembly time. Heat the tortillas, then add to the centre of each the spiced turkey, coriander rice, red cabbage, pineapple salsa, avo, hot sauce yoghurt and pickled jalapeños, if using. Fold over the ends and roll up to seal. Cut in half and enjoy.

Cauliflower *Salad with* **Green Tahini**

VG DF

The green tahini is what makes this dish. Think of your favourite lemony, velvety vegan dressing and then make it even better by adding fresh herbs, spring onions and green chilli. That, plus the textural contrast between the roasted and raw cauliflower, brings it all home. Pearled spelt is good for your digestive system and is also high in vitamins B and E, plus the addition of vitamin C-rich cauliflower makes this dish high in fibre.

Cook time: 1 hr

Ingredients

Serves 4

150g (5½oz) pearled spelt (or use quinoa or bulgar wheat instead)
100g (3½oz) radishes
3 lemons
2 large cauliflowers
2 tsp smoked paprika
2 tsp ground coriander
1 tsp ground cumin
3 tbsp olive oil
a large handful each of basil and mint
1 green chilli
4 spring onions
4 tbsp tahini
salt and black pepper

Method

1. Preheat the oven to 220°C/200°C fan/gas mark 7.

2. Cook the spelt or grain of your choice according to the packet instructions.

3. Finely slice your radishes, then add them to a bowl. Squeeze over the juice of 1 lemon, then leave to slightly pickle.

4. Cut 1½ cauliflowers into medium-sized florets and roughly chop the stalks and leaves too. Tip into your largest roasting tin, toss with the ground spices, plenty of seasoning and 2 tablespoons of the olive oil, then spread into a single layer so that they roast evenly. Roast for 20–25 minutes until tender and a little charred.

5. Meanwhile, very thinly slice the remaining cauliflower half and tip into your largest bowl. Pour in the remaining olive oil and squeeze in the juice of 1 lemon. Toss together and set aside – the lemon juice will soften the raw cauliflower slightly.

6. Green tahini time. Put most of the basil (stalks and all) and mint leaves into a blender. Roughly chop the green chilli (deseed it if you don't like it too hot) and 2 of the spring onions and add these to the blender along with the zest and juice of the remaining lemon, the tahini and 5 tablespoons of water. Blitz to a vivid green dressing of a thick drizzling consistency (add a splash more water if it needs loosening). Season to taste.

7. Come back to the grains: drain in a sieve, rinse, then shake off any excess water. Tip into the bowl with the raw cauliflower. Once the cauliflower is roasted, add this too. Gently fold everything together and season to taste.

8. Thinly slice the remaining spring onions (both green and white parts) and pick the remaining herbs. Divide the salad between four plates and drizzle over the green tahini dressing. Top with the spring onions, pickled radishes, herbs and serve.

Gochujang **Greens**

VG GF DF

The idea for this recipe came from having lots of random bits of veg in the fridge and not knowing quite what to do with them. The result? A spicy tangle of greens on a bed of fluffy rice. The ultimate shovel-it-in dinner. Leafy greens are a nutrition powerhouse, so we made sure to add plenty here.

Cook time: 45 mins

Ingredients

Serves 4

large thumb-sized piece of fresh ginger
3 garlic cloves
2–3 tbsp gochujang (depending on how spicy you like it)
2tsp cornflour
2 tbsp soy sauce
2 tbsp rapeseed oil
300g (10½oz) basmati rice
2 leeks
200g (7oz) tenderstem broccoli
200g (7oz) kale
200g (7oz) frozen peas
60g (2¼oz) roasted and salted peanuts
1 lime

Ingredient Hack: You can use whatever greens you fancy here.

Method

1. Finely grate three-quarters of the ginger and all the garlic into a small bowl, then add the gochujang, 2 teaspoons of cornflour and soy sauce. Stir until you have a smooth sauce, then set aside.

2. Cut the remaining ginger into fine matchsticks and coat in the remaining teaspoon of cornflour. Get a small frying pan over a high heat. Pour in 1 tablespoon of the rapeseed oil, add the coated ginger and fry until crisp. Set aside to cool.

3. Cook the rice according to the packet instructions.

4. Meanwhile, halve and thinly slice the leeks. Get a large frying pan over a medium heat, add the remaining tablespoon of rapeseed oil and tip in the leeks. Cook for 5 minutes until beginning to collapse and soften, then cut the broccoli into thirds and add to the pan.

5. Pour in 3 tablespoons of water, turn the heat up to high and cook for 2–3 minutes more until the broccoli is nearly tender and the water has evaporated. Strip the leaves off your kale into bite-size pieces, then add with the peas and give everything a good mix to combine. Once the kale starts wilting, pour in the gochujang sauce.

6. Cook for a couple of minutes more, stirring, so that all the veg gets coated in the sauce. It will thicken up and start to cling to the greens. You're now ready to serve.

7. Divide the rice between four bowls. Top with the gochujang greens, then roughly chop the peanuts and scatter them and the crispy ginger over the top. Serve with the lime, cut into wedges.

XO *Aubergine* **Salad**

GF DF

XO is a spicy seafood sauce that comes from Hong Kong. Traditionally made using dried shrimps, air-dried ham, garlic, ginger and soy, it's a real umami bomb. Here, we've simplified it slightly to create the most unreal dressing. This salad is dressed to impress.

Cook time: 50 mins

Ingredients

Serves 4

- 1 large aubergine
- 1 butternut squash
- 3 tbsp rapeseed oil
- 4 slices of serrano or Parma ham
- 1 banana shallot
- 3 garlic cloves
- thumb-sized piece of fresh ginger
- 2 tsp shrimp paste
- 2 tsp chilli flakes
- 1 tbsp soft light brown sugar
- 1 tbsp soy sauce
- 3 tbsp rice wine vinegar
- 1 red chilli
- 200g (7oz) sugar snap peas
- 4 spring onions
- a small bunch each of mint and coriander
- salt and black pepper

Gluten-Free: Use tamari instead of the soy sauce.

Method

1. Preheat the oven to 220°C/200°C fan/gas mark 7.

2. Cut the aubergine and butternut squash (no need to peel either) into roughly 2cm (¾in) pieces. Put into a bowl, add some seasoning and 2½ tablespoons of the rapeseed oil. Toss so that the veg gets evenly coated in the oil, then tip out into your largest roasting tin and spread into a single layer so that it cooks evenly. Roast for 35 minutes until cooked through and caramelized in places.

3. Meanwhile, make the dressing of champions. Finely chop the ham, shallot, garlic and ginger.

4. Get a saucepan over a medium heat. Pour in the remaining ½ tablespoon of rapeseed oil, add the ham and shallot and cook, stirring occasionally, until the shallot is soft and the ham crisp. Add the garlic, ginger, shrimp paste and chilli flakes and cook, stirring, for 2 minutes before adding the sugar and soy sauce. Remove from the heat and stir through the vinegar; set aside. The dressing should have a real funk: sharp, salty, sweet. All of the good stuff.

5. Thinly slice the chilli, sugar snaps and spring onions (both green and white parts). Pick the mint leaves, then roughly chop the coriander (stalks and all).

6. Pile the roasted aubergine and squash onto a serving platter, along with the chilli, sugar snaps, spring onions and herbs. Spoon over the dressing to serve.

Tofu Salad with *Miso & Tahini* **Dressing**

VG GF DF

If you've never tried miso and tahini together before then this ultra-silky umami dressing is going to blow you away. Tossed with a rainbow of raw veg high in phytochemicals (the good stuff) and crispy smoked tofu, this dish is freshness personified.

Cook time: 45 mins

Ingredients

Serves 4

1 small red cabbage
2 medium carrots
4 spring onions
2 peppers (red, yellow or orange)
100g (3½oz) frozen edamame beans (optional)
a small bunch each of mint and coriander
50g (1¾oz) roasted and salted cashews
thumb-sized piece of fresh ginger
2 limes
2 tbsp miso
3 tbsp tahini
450g (1lb) smoked tofu (we like The Tofoo Co)
1 tbsp coconut oil

Method

1. Very finely shred or coarsely grate the red cabbage and scrape into your largest bowl. Do the same with the carrots and add to the bowl. Thinly slice the spring onions (both green and white parts) and slice the peppers, then add to the bowl.

2. Pour boiling water over the edamame, if using; once defrosted drain into a sieve, shake off any excess water and tip into the salad bowl. Pick and tear the mint leaves, roughly chop the coriander (stalks and all) and scatter these on top of the salad. Roughly chop the cashews and add these too. Set the salad aside without mixing – yet.

3. Dressing time. Finely grate the ginger (no need to peel) into a small bowl. Zest in the limes, add the miso and tahini, then squeeze in the lime juice. Mix together, adding enough water to make it a drizzle-able consistency (about 4 tablespoons).

4. Next fry the tofu. Drain, then cut the tofu into cubes. Place a large frying pan over a medium–high heat and melt the coconut oil, then add the tofu cubes and fry, turning regularly, until evenly crisp and golden.

5. Assembly time. Pour the dressing into the salad, toss everything together, then divide between four bowls. Top with the crispy tofu to serve.

Spicy Coconut Yoghurt Soup *with Baked* **Pakoras**

VG GF DF

A riff on traditional Indian *khadi* – throwing pakoras into the fragrant soup gives it a unique, moreish texture. We baked the pakoras, using much less oil than frying. The dough will be very wet; this makes them more tender! Just make sure to line your tray with baking paper so they don't stick. Feel free to up the spice if you want.

Cook time: 50 mins

Ingredients

Serves 4

For the soup
350g (12oz) coconut yoghurt
50g (1¾oz) chickpea (gram) flour
½ onion
1 tbsp vegetable oil
1 tsp cumin seeds
1 lemon
1 tsp ground turmeric
2 tsp salt

For the baked pakoras
½ onion
2 medium potatoes
5cm (2in) piece of fresh ginger
2 garlic cloves
1 tsp salt
a small handful of coriander
3 green chillies
150g (5½oz) chickpea (gram) flour

For the tarka
6 garlic cloves
4 green chilies
2 tbsp vegetable oil
1 tbsp cumin seeds
1 sprig of curry leaves

Method

1. Preheat the oven to 180°C/160°C fan/gas mark 4 and line a baking tray with baking paper.

2. Start with the soup. In a large jug whisk together the yoghurt, chickpea flour and 500ml (17fl oz) of water. Dice the onion half.

3. Pour the vegetable oil into a large high-sided frying pan, place over a medium–high heat and add the cumin seeds. Add the onion and cook for 5 minutes until caramelized.

4. Add the yoghurt mixture and whisk in 1 litre (1¾ pints) of water. Bring to a bubble and continue to cook, while whisking, for 5 minutes – if it splits don't worry: just keep whisking and it will come back together. Season with the juice of the lemon, turmeric and salt, then let this bubble away over a low heat while you make your pakoras.

5. Grate the other onion half, potatoes (skin on), ginger and garlic into a large bowl. Sprinkle in the salt and mix well with your hands. Finely chop the coriander (stalks and all) and green chillies and mix in. Add the chickpea flour and form a thick but wet paste.

6. Using two tablespoons or your hands, form small balls (about the size of a ping-pong ball) and place onto the lined tray. Bake for 15–20 minutes until golden and crisp.

7. Meanwhile, for the tarka, thinly slice the garlic and cut the green chillies in half lengthways.

8. Once the pakoras are baked, add most of them to the soup, saving a few to garnish the top.

9. Heat the 2 tablespoons of vegetable oil in the smallest saucepan you have. Add the cumin seeds and the sliced garlic. Fry for 2 minutes over a low heat until the garlic is just starting to brown. Add the green chillies and after 30 seconds add the curry leaves. Once the curry leaves turn bright green, pour this all over the yoghurt soup and immediately cover with a lid. Let this infuse for 5 minutes before ladling into bowls and enjoying.

mob

Robyn's Sticky Aubergine **Rice Bowl**

VG GF DF

This is a recipe that Ben developed, and became obsessed with, during the first lockdown. It's the Holy Trinity of sticky, sweet and spicy. Give it a go, Mob, you won't regret it. Plus the variety of veg gives a great kick of fibre.

Cook time: 1 hr 15 mins

Ingredients

Serves 4

3 aubergines
1½ tbsp vegetable oil
a bunch of spring onions
½ red cabbage
4 garlic cloves
thumb-sized piece of fresh ginger
2 red chillies
1 lime
3 tbsp rice vinegar
1 tbsp sesame oil
320g (11¼oz) sushi rice
1 tbsp hoisin sauce
2 tbsp soy sauce
1 tbsp crispy chilli oil (we like Lee Kum Kee), separating the oil and crispy chilli
2 tbsp sesame seeds, plus extra to serve
1 tbsp agave nectar or maple syrup
1 vegetable stock cube
1 tbsp shichimi (use 2:1 chilli powder and salt)
1 avocado
salt

Gluten-free: Check the labels of the hoisin sauce and veg stock, and use tamari instead of soy sauce.

Cooking Hack: If you find your rice has stuck to the bottom of the pan once cooked, turn the heat off and leave the lid on and it will steam itself off.

Method

1. Preheat the oven to 170°C/150°C fan/gas mark 3.

2. Slice the aubergines into batons and whack them in a colander. Salt and leave for 5 minutes to extract the water. After 5 minutes, pat dry and get them onto a baking tray. Drizzle with 1 tablespoon of the vegetable oil and place in the oven for 30 minutes.

3. While your aubergine is roasting, prep your veg. Thinly slice the spring onions, red cabbage, garlic, ginger and red chillies.

4. Grab two bowls. Add the spring onions to one and the red cabbage to the other. Cover the spring onions with the juice of the lime, 1 tablespoon of the rice vinegar and a sprinkling of salt. Over the red cabbage pour another tablespoon of rice vinegar, ½ tablespoon of the sesame oil and a sprinkle of salt and mix it through. Cover and place both in the fridge.

5. Rinse the sushi rice, then add to a saucepan with just enough water to cover. Leave for 30 minutes to soak.

6. Heat the remaining ½ tablespoon of oil in a wok or large frying pan and add the garlic, ginger and red chillies and fry over a low heat. Once softened, add the hoisin sauce, soy sauce, the remaining ½ tablespoon of sesame oil and 1 tablespoon of rice vinegar, the chilli oil, sesame seeds, agave and veggie stock cube. Give everything a good mix together, then add the aubergine straight from the oven.

7. Add enough water to just cover the aubergine and leave to simmer until it has reduced into a lovely thick sauce. Stir often.

8. Drain the rice and add it to a saucepan with 480ml (16fl oz) water and the shichimi. Bring to the boil, then turn to a simmer, cover with the lid and simmer until cooked, about 15 minutes.

9. Time to plate up. First, make a bed of your sushi rice. Add a generous dollop of aubergine sauce, a helping of marinated red cabbage and some sliced avocado. Garnish with the spring onions, the crispy chilli bits from the chilli oil and some more sesame seeds and tuck in.

Charred Spring Onion *& Broccoli* Curry

VG GF DF 30

Although it's often relegated to the sidelines, we're using spring onion as a main veg here, cutting it into inch-sized pieces and charring it with some broccoli to add a smoky sweetness to this fragrant, coconut-forward curry. Broccoli, kale, lemon and cherry tomatoes all help boost the amount of vitamin C in this big vegan win that's just asking to become a weeknight staple.

Cook time: 30 mins

Ingredients

Serves 4

a bunch of spring onions
200g (2oz) tenderstem broccoli
4 tsp rapeseed oil
300g (10½oz) basmati rice
1 tbsp cumin seeds
1 tbsp mustard seeds
2 tsp fennel seeds (optional)
3 fat garlic cloves
2 tsp ground turmeric
2 tsp ground coriander
1–2 tsp chilli flakes (depending on how much spice you like), plus a pinch to serve
200g (7oz) cherry tomatoes
2 × 400ml (14fl oz) tins of coconut milk
100g (3½oz) kale
1 lemon
salt and black pepper

Method

1. Cut the spring onions (both green and white parts) and tenderstem broccoli into 3cm (1in) pieces. Add to a bowl, toss with plenty of salt and pepper and 2 teaspoons of the rapeseed oil.

2. Get a large, high-sided non-stick frying pan over a super-high heat. Working in batches, fry the veg until charred and tender. The broccoli will take around 3 minutes on each side, and the spring onions around a minute. Once charred, pile onto a plate and repeat until all the veg is charred.

3. Cook the basmati rice according to the packet instructions.

4. Meanwhile, put the frying pan back over a low-medium heat. Pour in the remaining rapeseed oil. Add the whole spices and toast until they pop. Crush in the garlic, cook for 30 seconds, then add the remaining spices. Mix, then chuck in the cherry tomatoes.

5. Pour in the coconut milk and bring the sauce to a simmer. Bubble away for 10 minutes until the tomatoes start to burst, then add the kale. Once it has wilted, take the curry off the heat. Season with salt, pepper and lemon juice to taste. Add the charred veg and leave without stirring for a couple of minutes to warm through.

6. Divide the rice and curry between four bowls and sprinkle over chilli flakes to serve.

Sticky Mango *Paneer* **Wraps**

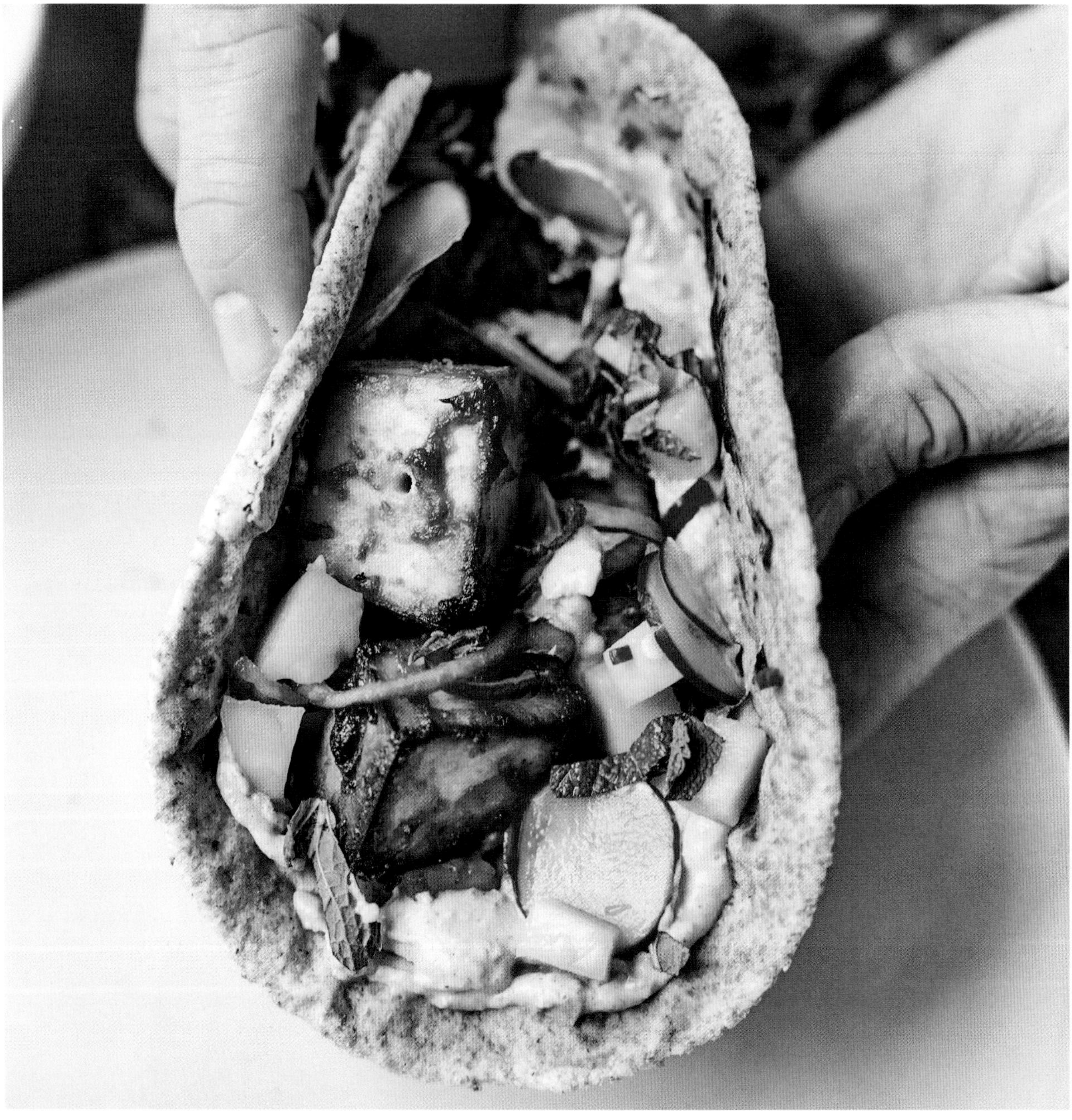

(V)

This is the ultimate vegetarian-friendly barbecue dish: zingy mango salsa is the perfect thing to serve with charred paneer, curry yoghurt, pickly bits and soft wraps. A crunchy pickle adds a good dose of nutrients and freshness to complement the stickiness. Don't feel like this is just for the summer, though, as you can enjoy this baby all year round.

Cook time: 1 hr

Ingredients

Serves 4

You will need 8 wooden skewers soaked in water

320g (11¼oz) paneer
1 red onion
100g (3½oz) radishes
4cm (1½in) piece of fresh ginger
4 garlic cloves
1 tsp ground cumin
½ tsp chilli powder
½ tsp ground turmeric
3 tbsp mango chutney
1 tbsp tomato purée
2 tbsp rapeseed oil
2 tbsp curry powder
1 lime
150g (5½oz) natural yoghurt
4 roti
1 mango
a handful of mint
1 red chilli
salt and black pepper

Method

1. Cut the paneer into large cubes and pop into a large bowl. Thinly slice the red onion and radishes and set aside.

2. Roughly chop the ginger and garlic. Add to a food processor along with the cumin, chilli powder and turmeric. Add 2 tablespoons of the mango chutney, the tomato purée, 1 tablespoon of rapeseed oil, 4 tablespoons of water and a good pinch of salt and pepper. Blend to a smooth paste. Pour over the paneer and toss to coat. Leave for at least 30 minutes, or more time if you have it.

3. Heat the remaining tablespoon of rapeseed oil in a frying pan set over a medium heat. Add half the onion and cook for 15 minutes until it is totally soft and starting to caramelize. Add the curry powder and cook for 2 minutes. Leave to cool a little.

4. Add the radishes to a bowl along with the remaining sliced onion. Squeeze over the lime juice and sprinkle in a good pinch of salt, then scrunch up with your hands to encourage the veg to pickle. Set aside.

5. Spoon the caramelized onions into the food processor. Add the yoghurt and the remaining tablespoon of mango chutney, then blitz until totally smooth.

6. Heat your barbecue or grill to a medium–high heat. Skewer the paneer pieces onto the skewers. If grilling, arrange on a baking tray and grill for 6 minutes on each side, turning until evenly cooked and starting to char around the edges. If barbecuing, place on the grills and cook the paneer in the same way.

7. Warm the roti up in the oven according to the packet instructions.

8. Peel and finely dice the mango, roughly chop the mint leaves and dice the chilli. Mix together in a bowl with a pinch of salt.

9. Assembly time. Spread a little of the yoghurt on each roti, then add the mango kachumber. Slide the paneer off the skewers on to the roti, then add the pickled radishes. Serve and enjoy.

mob

Soy, Ginger *& Lime* **Nutty salad**

VG DF

Magic happens when you combine a zippy salad dressing with a handful of nuts, which add a healthy source of fat – necessary for absorbing fat-soluble vitamins. Heavy on the ginger and lime, this bright and crunchy salad is a great way to wake up your palate. The perfect meal prep recipe for anyone that hates meal prep.

Cook time: 35 mins

Ingredients

Serves 4

100g (3½oz) mixed nuts
1 tbsp medium curry powder
1 large head of broccoli
200g (7oz) green beans
200g (7oz) frozen edamame beans
150g (5½oz) bulgar wheat and quinoa mix (or use straight quinoa instead)
2 limes
thumb-sized piece of fresh ginger
3 tbsp olive oil
3 tbsp soy sauce
2 tsp maple syrup
2 carrots
salt and black pepper

Method

1. Preheat the oven to 180°C/160°C fan/gas mark 4. Bring a large saucepan of water to the boil.

2. Tip the nuts onto a baking tray, toss with the curry powder and plenty of seasoning. Spread into an even layer and roast for 6–8 minutes until nicely toasted. Set aside.

3. Meanwhile, cut the broccoli into smallish florets and dice the stalk. Cut the green beans in half. Drop the broccoli and beans into the saucepan of water, bring back to the boil and cook for 2 minutes, then add the edamame and cook for about 1 minute more – you want everything to be just cooked with a nice crunch. Drain into a colander and set aside to cool.

4. Cook the bulgar and quinoa mix according to the packet instructions.

5. Dressing time. Zest the limes into a large bowl, finely grate in the ginger (no need to peel), then add the olive oil, soy sauce and maple syrup. Squeeze in the lime juice, then season to taste. Peel and dice the carrots and add to the bowl.

6. Drain and rinse the cooked bulgar and quinoa into a sieve, then shake off any water and tip into the dressing bowl.

7. Add the cooked greens to the bowl. Roughly chop the nuts (or leave them whole if you can't be bothered) and add these too, along with any curry powder from the tray. Toss everything together so that it gets coated in the dressing, then dish up and enjoy.

Tamarind & Tomato *Salmon* **Curry**

GF DF

This lively little curry couldn't be simpler. Blitz up your own curry paste, add a few tins of cherry tomatoes for sweetness, then finish with some tamarind – its tanginess works perfectly with the unctuous salmon. Salmon is a great source of omega-3 fatty acids which, along with turmeric and ginger, has anti-inflammatory properties.

Cook time: 40 mins

Ingredients

Serves 4

1 onion
thumb-sized piece of fresh ginger
1–2 red chillies (depending on how spicy you like it)
a large handful of coriander
3 garlic cloves
2 tsp ground turmeric
1 tbsp rapeseed oil
1 tbsp cumin seeds
1 tbsp mustard seeds
2 × 400g (14oz) tins of cherry tomatoes
300g (10½oz) basmati rice
4 skinless and boneless salmon fillets
200g (7oz) green beans
2 tbsp tamarind paste
salt and black pepper

Method

1. Roughly chop the onion, ginger and chilli (deseeding if you like). Cut the coriander stalks away from the leaves, saving the leaves.

2. Put the onion, ginger, chilli, coriander stalks, garlic, turmeric and 3 tablespoons of water into a food processor and blitz to a smoothish curry paste, adding a little more water if it needs it.

3. Get a large frying pan or saucepan (one that has a lid) over a medium heat. Pour in the rapeseed oil, then scrape in the curry paste. Cook, stirring occasionally, for about 5 minutes until the raw onion has cooked out and the water has evaporated. Add the cumin and mustard seeds, cook for 1 minute more, then tip in the tomatoes.

4. Simmer the curry for 10 minutes, popping a few of the whole cherry tomatoes with the back of your spoon. Start cooking the rice according to the packet instructions.

5. Next, season the salmon fillets and cut into large chunks. Cut the green beans in half.

6. Add the tamarind paste to the curry, then season to taste. Stir through the green beans and place the pieces of salmon on top. Put a lid on the pan and cook for 5–6 minutes until the fish is just cooked through – it will flake into large chunks.

7. Scatter the coriander leaves over the curry and serve in the middle of the table along with the rice for people to help themselves.

Gingery Chicken Broth *with Crispy* **Chicken Skin**

DF

We think this might be most heart-warming soup we've ever eaten. The richness of the crispy chicken skin and chilli oil contrast wonderfully with the lightness of the gingery broth. We've packed this recipe with garlic, making it high in antioxidants and anti-inflammatory properties. You'll want seconds of this one, trust us.

Cook time: 2 hrs 30 mins

Ingredients

Serves 4

1.2kg (2lb 10oz) whole chicken
3 bunches of spring onions
50g (1¾oz) fresh ginger
1½ garlic bulbs
2 tbsp vegetable oil
4 red chillies
a large pinch of flaky sea salt
a small bunch of coriander
400g (14oz) udon noodles
4 tbsp soy sauce
2 tsp ground white pepper

Cooking Hack: Use any leftover chicken stock to cook rice – it will be some of the best rice you will ever eat!

Method

1. Remove the skin from chicken and snip it up into small bits – using a pair of cooking scissors helps to cut through any thick fat. Roughly chop up 2 bunches of spring onions and three-quarters of the ginger (no need to peel). Slice a whole garlic bulb in half.

2. Pour 1 tablespoon of vegetable oil into your largest saucepan and add half of the chopped spring onions along with the chopped ginger and one half of your garlic bulb. Gently cook over a lowish heat for 2 minutes until fragrant but before it takes on any colour.

3. Add in the whole skinned chicken and enough cold water to cover the chicken. Add the remaining chopped spring onions and simmer for 1 hour until the chicken is cooked.

4. Take the chicken out of the pan of stock. When cool enough to handle, shred the meat off the carcass and set aside. Return the bones to the stock, then simmer over a gentle heat for as long as you can. It will need 1 hour at the very least.

5. Bash up the cloves from the remaining ½ garlic bulb in a pestle and mortar with the remaining ginger (peeled this time), the red chillies and sea salt to form a chunky paste.

6. Add the chicken fat and remaining tablespoon of vegetable oil to a saucepan and fry over a very low heat for 5 minutes until golden and crispy. Add the chilli paste and cook for 10 minutes over a very low heat until the skin is crispy and the oil is stained red.

7. Meanwhile, finely chop the remaining spring onions and the coriander.

8. Cook the udon noodles in hot water (follow the packet instructions).

9. Strain the soup, add in the shredded chicken and season with the soy sauce and white pepper.

10. Divide the udon between four bowls. Pour over the soup and top with the chopped spring onions and coriander and the chilli sauce. Enjoy.

WEEKEND

Steak *with Blue Cheese* **Salad**

GF

This is our take on a steakhouse classic but with a blend of indulgence and nourishment, balancing the cheese with plenty of beetroot and radish to nourish your gut microbiome. We've used bavette – a delicious, lesser-known cut of meat that's popular in French bistros. It pairs excellently with shallots and an earthy beetroot and blue cheese salad.

Cook time: 1 hr 20 mins

Ingredients

Serves 4

500g (1lb 2oz) beetroot
6 banana shallots
4 tbsp olive oil, plus 2 tsp
300ml (10½fl oz) chicken stock
a few sprigs of thyme
60g (2¼oz) walnuts
2 tbsp honey, plus 1 tsp
4 tbsp balsamic vinegar (get the best quality you can afford)
2 red chicory
200g (7oz) radishes
1 lemon
100g (3½oz) blue cheese (we like Saint Agur)
600g (1lb 5oz) bavette steak
salt and black pepper

Ingredient Hack: If you can't find bavette, use for 2 large sirloin steaks instead, reducing the cooking time to 2–2½ minutes on each side.

Method

1. Preheat the oven to 220°C/200°C fan/gas mark 7.

2. Wash the beetroot, then wrap individually in foil, seasoning with salt and pepper. Put into a roasting tin and roast for 45 minutes–1 hour, depending on size, until completely tender.

3. Next, cut each shallot in half lengthways. Put into a large bowl, toss with 2 tablespoons of the olive oil and plenty of seasoning.

4. Get your largest frying pan over a medium–high heat. Add the shallots, cut-side down and fry until the underside is nicely charred – about 5 minutes. Once charred, snugly place charred-side upright into a roasting tin, then pour over the stock, strip in the thyme leaves and cover tightly with foil. Roast in the oven for 30 minutes.

5. Meanwhile, roughly chop the walnuts, put into the same frying pan and toast over a medium heat until turning golden, then drizzle over 1 teaspoon of the honey, tossing until they are sticky and caramelized. Tip into a bowl and set aside to cool.

6. After 30 minutes come back to the shallots. Add the remaining honey and the balsamic vinegar. Return to the oven, uncovered, for a further 30 minutes until soft, sticky and caramelized in sauce.

7. Meanwhile, make your salad. Peel the cooked beetroot (the skin will come off easily), then cut into wedges. Separate the chicory leaves, thinly slice the radishes and put everything onto a platter. Squeeze over the lemon juice, season and drizzle over the remaining 2 tablespoons of olive oil. Crumble over the blue cheese and scatter over the honeyed walnuts.

8. Steak time. Get your largest frying pan over a high heat. Wait until it is searing hot. Season the bavette generously with salt and pepper, then rub on both sides with the remaining 2 teaspoons of olive oil. Add to the hot pan and fry for 4–4½ minutes on each side until cooked until your liking. Put onto a plate to rest.

9. Slice the steak, then lay on a serving plate with the caramelized shallots in their sauce and the salad alongside.

Mushroom Burgers *with Apple* Chutney

VG

We went classic British gastropub vibes with this mushroom veggie burger. The lentils and mushrooms are packed with fibre and protein. We've used brown sauce to create a quick apple chutney and lobbed in some Marmite and Cheddar for a big boost of umami. The meaty texture of the mushrooms will make it a hit with meat eaters and vegetarians alike.

Cook time: 50 mins

Ingredients

Serves 4

1 onion
2 tbsp olive oil
1 red chilli
2 small apples
2 tbsp brown sauce
2 tbsp apple cider vinegar
1 × 400g (14oz) tin of green lentils
200g (7oz) mixed mushrooms
2 tsp smoked paprika
2 tsp Marmite
1 fat garlic clove
a handful of thyme sprigs
75g (2¾oz) panko breadcrumbs
100g (3½oz) extra mature Cheddar cheese
4 brioche or seeded burger buns
4 tbsp crispy onions
4 handfuls of watercress
potato wedges and a side salad, to serve (optional)

Make it Vegan/Dairy-Free: Use vegan cheese.

Method

1. First make the cheat's chutney. Finely chop the onion and scrape into a saucepan over a medium heat. Pour in 1 tablespoon of the oil and cook the onion until is soft, stirring occasionally.

2. Meanwhile, finely chop the red chilli and peel, core and dice the apples into small cubes.

3. Once the onion is soft, scrape half into a bowl to be used later. Add the chilli and the apples to the pan. Give everything a good stir to combine, then spoon in the brown sauce and apple cider vinegar, along with 3 tablespoons of water. Cook, stirring occasionally, until the apples are softened but holding their shape and the sauce has thickened. Set aside to cool.

4. While the chutney is cooking, make the burger patties. Drain the lentils into a sieve, shaking off any excess water. Put the mushrooms into a food processor and blitz until very finely chopped. Tip in the lentils, then add the bowl of cooked onion, smoked paprika and Marmite. Crush in the garlic clove, strip in the thyme leaves from the sprigs and add the breadcrumbs, then briefly pulse until the mixture comes together. Shape into four burger patties and leave to cool in the fridge.

5. Preheat the grill to high. Get a large non-stick frying pan over a medium–high heat. Pour in the remaining tablespoon of olive oil and lay in the burgers. Cook for 3–4 minutes on each side until

well crusted and cooked through, carefully flipping with a spatula halfway. Transfer to a baking tray, grate over the cheese then slide under the grill for a minute or so until the cheese is melted.

6. Assembly time. Halve the buns and toast in the pan, then layer in the mushroom burger, apple chutney, crispy onions and watercress and sandwich together. We like to eat this with some potato wedges and a side salad.

Curried *Clam* **Noodles**

GF **DF** 30

One of our recipe testers only managed to take a picture of this AFTER it had already been eaten by everyone. Clams are not only a lean source of protein but also rich in vitamins and minerals such as zinc. Cooking clams couldn't be easier, and their sweet meat pairs perfectly with the coconut sauce and rice noodles – kind of like a bastardized vongole.

Cook time: 30 minutes

Ingredients

Serves 4

1kg (2lb 4oz) clams
250g (9oz) flat rice noodles
2 banana shallots
3 fat garlic cloves
thumb-sized piece of fresh ginger
a large handful of coriander
1 tbsp rapeseed oil
1 tsp ground turmeric
2 tsp curry powder
2 tsp ground cumin
1 tsp chilli powder
1 × 400ml (14fl oz) tin of coconut milk
2 pak choi
1 lime
salt and black pepper

Ingredient Hack: If you prefer mussels, use them instead, cooking for 1–2 minutes longer until all the shells have opened.

Method

1. Give the clams a rinse in a bowl of cold water, discarding any that have broken shells and don't stay shut when you squeeze them tightly in the palm of your hand. Drain into a colander, then tip back into the bowl and keep in the fridge while you prep.

2. Get a kettle on to boil. Put the rice noodles into a large bowl, pour over the boiling water and leave for about 10 minutes, or until softened.

3. Finely chop the shallots, garlic, ginger and coriander stalks. Get your largest saucepan (one with a tight-fitting lid) over a medium heat. Pour in the rapeseed oil and add the shallots, along with a pinch of salt. Cook, stirring occasionally, until soft. Add the garlic, ginger and coriander stalks, cook for 1 minute, then spoon in the ground spices.

4. Give everything a good mix to combine, cook for 30 seconds more until smelling amazing, then pour in the coconut milk. Turn up the heat to medium–high and bring the sauce to the boil.

5. Once boiling, tip in the clams. Immediately put a lid on the pan and cook, shaking the pan occasionally, for 3–4 minutes until all the clams have opened.

6. Meanwhile, very thinly slice the pak choi and roughly chop the coriander leaves. Drain the noodles into a sieve.

7. Once the clams have opened, add the noodles, pak choi and most of the coriander leaves. Give everything a good toss to combine, cook for a further minute until the pak choi have just wilted, then squeeze in the lime juice. Season to taste.

8. Divide the curried clam noodles between four bowls and scatter over the remaining coriander to serve.

Hot *Tofu* **Satay**

VG GF DF

This is our version of a Malaysian street-food snack. We've loaded it with bold anti-inflammatory spices, which, when combined with a fresh cucumber pickle, help aid digestion and boosts your immune system. Serving it with our delicious peanut sauce and pickled vegetables is non-negotiable.

Cook time: 1 hr

Ingredients

Serves 4

You will need a packet of wooden skewers (about 25–30) to trim to your desired length. Soak them in water for 30 minutes before you start.

For the pickle

½ cucumber
1 red onion
300ml (10½fl oz) apple cider vinegar
1 tsp salt
1 tbsp sugar

For the skewers

400g (14oz) firm tofu
2 garlic cloves
1 banana shallot
1 lemongrass stalk
1 tsp ground coriander
1 tsp ground turmeric
1 tsp chilli powder
2 tbsp vegetable oil
1 red chilli
a small handful of coriander
50g (1¾oz) unsalted peanuts

For the satay sauce

2 garlic cloves
1 banana shallot
1 tbsp vegetable oil
¼ tsp chilli powder
½ tsp ground turmeric
¼ tsp ground coriander
3 tbsp tamarind paste
40g (1½oz) brown sugar
½ tsp salt
110g (4oz) crunchy peanut butter
200ml (7fl oz) coconut milk
2 tbsp dark soy sauce

Cooking Hack: Make an extra batch of satay sauce if you want; it will keep in the fridge for a good few weeks.

Gluten-Free: Use tamari in place of soy sauce.

Method

1. First make the pickle. Chop the cucumber in half lengthways and remove the seedy core, then thinly slice the cucumber and red onion and add them to a jar or deep bowl. Add the apple cider vinegar to a saucepan and bring to a simmer over a medium heat. Add the salt and sugar, mixing well until they dissolve. Pour the pickling mixture over the sliced cucumber and red onion and let them sit for 30 minutes.

2. Now for the tofu skewers. Roughly chop the tofu into 3cm (1¼in) cubes and add to a bowl.

3. Roughly chop the garlic, shallot and the white of your lemongrass (saving the green part for later) and add to a blender along with the ground coriander, ground turmeric and chilli powder. Add a splash of water and blend until smooth. Add this marinade to the bowl of tofu and mix thoroughly, then set aside.

4. Meanwhile, make the satay sauce. Start by very finely chopping the garlic and shallot. Get a saucepan over a medium heat, then add the vegetable oil and your chopped shallot and garlic. Fry for a few minutes until the veg is golden.

5. Add the chilli powder, ground turmeric and coriander to the pan and mix well. Next, you're going to want to go in with the tamarind paste, sugar, salt, peanut butter and the green parts of the lemongrass you chopped up earlier. Pour in 180ml (6fl oz) of water along with the coconut milk and soy sauce. Bring to the boil, making sure to regularly stir it so the bottom of the pan doesn't burn. This will take about 5 minutes. Turn the heat down and let it simmer for 30 minutes.

6. Preheat the grill to medium–high.

7. Thread 3 or 4 marinated tofu cubes onto each of your skewers (depending on size and personal preference).

8. Get a griddle pan hot over a medium–high heat. Lightly brush your tofu skewers with vegetable oil and add a few to the pan at a time, making sure not to overcrowd them. Cook each batch for a few minutes on each side until you get nice char lines.

9. Once they've got a nice bit of colour, pop your skewers under the hot grill for 10 minutes to finish them off. Meanwhile, thinly slice the red chilli, chop the coriander and crush the peanuts in a pestle and mortar.

10. Serve the tofu skewers with the satay sauce and pickled cucumber and red onion. Garnish with the sliced red chilli, chopped coriander and crushed peanuts.

One-Tray *Thai Green* Chicken

GF DF

This traybake curry method is going to change your life. The green curry paste is quick to throw together, then cooked down with crispy chicken legs in a roasting dish to make a banging dinner. The paste can be kept in the fridge for 3 days, or can even be kept in the freezer for 3 months.

Cook time: 1hr 15 mins

Ingredients

Serves 4

3 shallots
3 lemongrass stalks
3 green chillies
3 garlic cloves
2cm (¾in) piece of fresh ginger
a bunch of coriander
2 limes
1 tbsp coconut oil
4 chicken legs
1 × 400ml (14fl oz) tin of coconut milk
200ml (7fl oz) chicken stock
250g (9oz) pre-cooked brown rice
125g (4½oz) green beans
125g (4½oz) mangetout
1 red chilli
1 tsp soft brown sugar
2 tbsp fish sauce
salt

Ingredient Hack: Use a pouch of pre-cooked brown rice for ease.

Cooking Hack: You can use a pestle and mortar if you don't have a food processor.

Gluten-Free: Use gluten-free stock.

Method

1. Preheat the oven to 200°C/180°C fan/gas mark 6.

2. Roughly chop the shallots, lemongrass, chillies, garlic, ginger and half the coriander (stalks and all), then add everything to a food processor along with the grated zest of 1 of the limes and the coconut oil. Blitz to a rough purée. Set this curry paste aside.

3. Place a large roasting tray over a medium heat on the hob. Add the chicken legs to the tray, skin-side down, and cook for 5 minutes until they are deeply crispy and the fat has rendered out. Remove from the tray and set aside.

4. Add the green curry paste to the tray and cook for 3 minutes until fragrant. Tip in the coconut milk and chicken stock, then bring to a simmer. Return the chicken legs to the pan, then pop in the oven for 40 minutes.

5. After 40 minutes, remove the tray from the oven and stir in the cooked brown rice and veg, then return to the oven for another 5 minutes. Meanwhile, cut both limes into wedges, thinly slice the red chilli and roughly chop the rest of the coriander (stalks and all).

6. Add the brown sugar and fish sauce to the curry and stir to combine, then season to taste with salt. Scatter over the coriander and red chillies, and squeeze over your lime juice. Serve and enjoy.

’Nduja Seafood Stew *with Charred* **Spring Onions**

DF 30

Even if you're not super-confident cooking seafood, we're sure you'll be able to nail this dish. A combination of seafood makes this dish full of desirable fatty acids and high in protein. The squid, prawns and mussels cook quickly in the spicy 'nduja broth while a scattering of fresh herbs bumps up the brightness. Serve with crusty bread.

Cook time: 30 mins

Ingredients

Serves 4

1 litre (1¾ pints) fish stock
400g (14oz) raw shell-on king prawns
1 onion
1 red pepper
6 garlic cloves
a bunch of spring onions
1 tbsp olive oil
75g (2¾oz) tomato purée
100g (3½oz) 'nduja
250ml (9fl oz) white wine
400g (14oz) squid rings
400g (14oz) mussels
a handful of parsley
1 lemon
salt
sourdough bread, to serve

Ingredient Hack: If you can't get hold of shell-on prawns, don't worry; peeled raw prawns will work just as well here. Just make sure you season your stock.

Method

1. Pour the fish stock into a saucepan and place over a low heat. Add any vegetable and fish trimmings to the pan as you prep.

2. Peel the prawns and add the shells to the fish stock. Finely chop the onion, pepper and garlic.

3. Char the spring onions straight over the flame of a gas hob until dark and smoky; alternatively, you can do this in a hot griddle pan. Chop the charred spring onions into chunks.

4. Heat the olive oil in a large frying pan and add the chopped onion and pepper and a pinch of salt. Cook for 5 minutes over a high heat until softened and translucent.

5. Add the tomato purée and cook for 5 minutes until darkened in colour, then add the 'nduja and garlic and cook for another 2 minutes until the 'nduja has darkened a little and broken up slightly.

6. Pour the wine into the pan to deglaze, scraping up any bits at the bottom.

7. Strain the fish stock and add to the pan along with the charred spring onions and bring to a gentle simmer.

8. Add the prawns, squid and mussels, cover with a lid and turn off the heat. Allow to cook in the residual heat for 5 minutes. Meanwhile, roughly chop the parsley (stalks and all).

9. Check all the mussels have opened (discard any that remain closed), then add a squeeze of lemon juice and sprinkle over the charred spring onions and some parsley before serving with sourdough bread.

Baked Miso *Chicken Schnitzel with* **Kimchi Mayo**

DF

Marinating the chicken overnight in miso gives it a deep umami flavour that – once coated and baked with the crispy breadcrumbs and paired with a moreish kimchi mayo and soft-boiled egg – is hard to beat. We've baked the chicken instead of deep-frying it, using much less oil and making this dish much fresher.

Cook time: 40 mins + marinating time

Ingredients

Serves 4

4 skinless chicken breast fillets
4 tbsp miso
100g (3½oz) panko breadcrumbs
3 tbsp sesame seeds
4 tsp rapeseed oil
250g (9oz) kimchi
4 tbsp mayonnaise
1 tbsp hot sauce (we like sriracha)
4 medium eggs
½ red cabbage
80g (2¾oz) watercress
2 tbsp rice wine vinegar
salt and black pepper

Fancy Hack: If you can use a mixture of black and white sesame seeds this will look amazing.

Method

1. The day before, tear off a large piece of baking paper and place onto the work surface. Place two of the chicken breasts onto the paper, a few centimetres apart from each other, and place another sheet of baking paper on top. Use a rolling pin to satisfyingly bash the chicken to tenderize and flatten it to an even thickness – about 1½cm (⅝in). Repeat with the other two chicken breasts.

2. Add the miso to a large bowl. Pour in 3 tablespoons of water and whisk to a thin paste – you want it to just cling to the chicken. Add the chicken to the bowl and rub in so that each breast gets evenly coated in the marinade. Cover and put in the fridge overnight.

3. The next day preheat the oven to 220°C/200°C fan/gas mark 7. Place a wire rack over a large roasting tin, or better yet find a grill pan. Get the chicken out of the fridge.

4. Mix the panko, sesame seeds and a generous pinch of salt together in a wide bowl. One at a time, coat the marinated chicken breasts completely in the breadcrumbs. Place onto the wire rack/grill pan set-up – this is the secret to avoiding a soggy schnitzel bottom. Drizzle 1 teaspoon of oil evenly across each schnitzel. Roast in the oven for 25 minutes until golden brown and the chicken is cooked through.

5. Meanwhile, make the sides. For the kimchi mayo, finely chop 50g (1¾oz) of the kimchi. Mix together with the mayonnaise and hot sauce in a small bowl and season to taste. Bring a small saucepan of water to the boil. Drop in the eggs and cook for 6 minutes – set a timer as you want them runny. Once cooked, drain, cool slightly under the cold tap and then peel. Shred the red cabbage and toss with the watercress, the rice wine vinegar and some salt and pepper.

6. Assembly time. Divide the chicken schnitzel between four plates, along with a pile of veg, a dollop of kimchi mayo and the kimchi itself. Halve the eggs to serve for the ultimate dinner.

Chermoula Cod *Rolls with* **Harissa Yoghurt**

This sandwich is packed with bold, brash flavours. Chermoula is a North African sauce made with fresh herbs and cumin that pairs beautifully with grilled fish. So we've done just that. Packed into a crusty roll with harissa yoghurt, this is going to be your new favourite sandwich.

Cook time: 40 mins

Ingredients

Serves 4

2 tsp smoked paprika
1 tsp ground turmeric
1 tbsp olive oil
500g (1lb 2oz) skinless and boneless cod loin
150g (5½oz) thick Greek yoghurt
2 tbsp harissa (we like rose)
4 ciabatta rolls

For the chermoula

1 tsp cumin seeds
1 green chilli
30g (1oz) parsley
30g (1oz) coriander
2 tbsp olive oil
1 lemon
salt

Method

1. Combine the paprika and turmeric in a bowl with a good pinch of salt and the tablespoon of olive oil. Give it a mix.

2. Cut the cod loin into eight evenly sized pieces, then add to the bowl and toss with your hands to get it totally coated in the mixture. Pop it into the fridge to marinate for 20 minutes.

3. Meanwhile, make the chermoula. Toast the cumin seeds in a small dry frying pan for 2 minutes over a medium heat until fragrant. Roughly chop the green chilli.

4. Tip the cumin seeds into a blender along with the chilli, all of your parsley and coriander (stalks and all), the olive oil and 2 tablespoons of water. Squeeze in the juice from the lemon, then whizz to a smooth consistency. Season to taste with salt.

5. Spoon the yoghurt and harissa into a bowl, then mix to combine.

6. Preheat the grill to high and line a baking tray with baking paper.

7. Arrange the cod pieces on the lined tray, then place under the grill for 5 minutes. Carefully flip them over, then grill for another 2 minutes. The fish will be visibly flaky when it is cooked.

8. Halve the ciabatta rolls, then toast them over a medium–high heat in a dry frying pan until crisp.

9. Spread the base of each roll with the harissa mayo, then place two pieces of fish on top. Spoon over some chermoula, then top with the lid of your bun. Serve and enjoy.

Braised Chicken *with* Beans

GF DF 30

A one-pot wonder that requires minimal washing up and delivers maximum flavour, with the chicken and veggies creating a flavoursome broth. We've snuck kale in as a good source of iron, and the vitamin C from the lemon and parsley helps our bodies absorb it. Great with a bread for mopping up the juices.

Cook time: 30 mins

Ingredients

Serves 4

4 skin-on, bone-in chicken thighs
1 red onion
3 garlic cloves
200g (7oz) kale
½ tsp chilli flakes
2 × 400g (14oz) tins of butter beans
500ml (17fl oz) boiling chicken stock
1 lemon
a handful of parsley
salt and black pepper

Gluten-Free: Use gluten-free stock.

Method

1. Preheat the oven to 200°C/180°C fan/gas mark 6.

2. Season the chicken thighs all over with salt and place skin-side down into a large high-sided frying pan. Place over a medium–high heat and fry until the chicken has rendered some of the fat and the skin is golden brown, about 7–8 minutes.

3. Meanwhile, thinly slice the red onion and garlic and wash and roughly chop the kale.

4. Remove the chicken from the pan and set aside, on a plate, skin-side up.

5. Add the onion to the fat in the pan and cook gently over a medium heat for a few minutes until soft but not brown. Add the garlic and chilli flakes and cook for another 2 minutes.

6. Drain the butter beans and add to the pan along with the kale, chicken stock and the juice of the lemon. Mix well, then pour into a deep roasting tin.

7. Add the thighs back to the tray, skin-side up, so that the bottom half is submerged in the veggies and stock. Place into the oven for about 12–15 minutes until the chicken is cooked through – the juices will run clear when you insert a knife into the chicken. Meanwhile, roughly chop the parsley.

8. Divide the broth and veg between shallow bowls and top each with a crispy chicken thigh and some parsley.

Parmesan Cauliflower Steaks *with Pistachio* **Pesto**

V **GF**

This dish is a beautifully simple way of using up the entirety of a cauliflower to add fibre and vitamin C. Served with a gorgeous cauliflower leaf and pistachio pesto, it's all about low waste and high flavour.

Cook time: 45 mins

Ingredients

Serves 2

2 large cauliflowers
4 tsp olive oil, plus 4 tbsp
75g (2¾oz) Parmesan (or vegetarian alternative)
a large bunch of basil
60g (2¼oz) pistachios
1 lemon
2 red chillies
salt and black pepper
side salad, to serve

Make it Vegetarian: By using a vegetarian alternative to Parmesan.

Cooking Hacks: Hold back half of your cauliflower trimmings and leaves to use on another occasion.

Try not to move your cauliflower steaks around too much once you've cut them – they are delicate and can break easily.

Method

1. Preheat the oven to 200°C/180°C fan/gas mark 6.

2. Cut the leaves off the cauliflowers, then cut each one vertically down the middle of its stalk. Trim away the edges so that you end up with four steaks. Save the cauliflower leaves and the offcuts/scraps.

3. Place the cauliflower steaks onto a baking tray and rub each one with salt, pepper and 1 teaspoon of olive oil. Roast for 30 minutes, then remove from the oven and flip them over. Grate 45g (1½oz) of the Parmesan over the steaks, then return to the oven for 10 minutes.

4. Meanwhile, finely chop the cauliflower leaves.

5. Bring a saucepan of water to the boil. Add salt, then tip in the scraps of cauliflower and the leaves. Simmer for 5 minutes until tender, then drain and allow to cool.

6. Add the cooled cauliflower pieces and leaves to a food processor along with the basil, two-thirds of the pistachios and the remaining Parmesan, then blitz until you have a smooth paste. Add the 4 tablespoons of olive oil and the juice of the lemon then blitz again; stir in just enough water to make the sauce a drizzle-able consistency. Season to taste with salt and pepper.

7. Toast the remaining pistachios in a dry frying pan over a medium heat until smelling toasty, then finely chop them. Thinly slice the chillies.

8. Arrange the cauliflower steaks on two plates. Drizzle with the pesto, then sprinkle with the sliced chillies and chopped pistachios. Serve and enjoy.

Lemony Olive *Braised* Chicken

GF DF

A super-simple and super lemony chicken that's based on one of our favourite dishes ever: preserved lemon and olive tagine. the combination of lemon, turmeric and garlic makes this full of antioxidants. This easy-to-follow recipe is great for trying out some ingredients you might not have ever used before.

Cook time: 45 mins

Ingredients

Serves 4

1 tbsp olive oil
1kg (2lb 4oz) skin-on, bone-in chicken thighs
1 onion
8 garlic cloves
3 lemons
15 Kalamata olives
1 tbsp black peppercorns
1 tsp ground turmeric
100ml (3½fl oz) white wine
500ml (17fl oz) chicken stock
a small handful of parsley
salt and black pepper
crusty bread, to serve

Method

1. Pour the olive oil into a heavy-based saucepan and place over the lowest heat. Add the chicken thighs, skin-side down (you may need to do this in batches). Cook for 10 minutes until the chicken skin is very crispy and the fat has rendered out. Remove the chicken and set aside on a plate.

2. Meanwhile, dice the onion and slice the garlic. Zest and juice 2 of the lemons (you want 100ml/3½fl oz of lemon juice) and thinly slice the third lemon. Break apart the olives with your fingers, removing the stones.

3. Add the onion to the chicken fat and cook for 5 minutes over a medium–high heat until lightly golden. Add the garlic, black peppercorns and turmeric and cook for 2 minutes more.

4. Pour in the white wine to deglaze the pan and let the alcohol cook off for 5 minutes, or until the onions are sticky.

5. Return the chicken pieces to the pan along with the chicken stock, lemon zest and juice, lemon slices and olives. Cover and cook for 15 minutes until the chicken is cooked through.

6. Meanwhile, roughly chop the parsley (stalks and all).

7. Season with salt and black pepper and sprinkle with the parsley before serving with warm crusty bread. Enjoy!

Courgette, Tomato *& Fennel* **Gratin**

V

You can't beat the comfort of a cheesy breadcrumb-topped gratin, especially when it's packed full of garlicky, caramelized veg. We've made this more gut-friendly by swapping heavy cream for ricotta and adding plenty of veg. The rich tomato and basil sauce pairs extremely well with the creamy ricotta.

Cook time: 1 hr

Ingredients

Serves 4

1 tsp fennel seeds
5 garlic cloves
3 tbsp olive oil
1 × 400g (14oz) tin of chopped tomatoes
2 bunches of basil
3 fennel bulbs
6 courgettes
250g (9oz) ricotta
1 lemon
20g (¾oz) Parmesan (or vegetarian alternative)
4 tbsp breadcrumbs
salt and black pepper
rocket salad and warm focaccia, to serve

Method

1. Toast the fennel seeds in a dry pan until fragrant, then grind to a coarse powder in a pestle and mortar.

2. Finely grate the garlic and add to a cold saucepan with 1 tablespoon of the olive oil. Set the pan over a medium heat and cook until the garlic just starts to brown.

3. Season with salt and pepper, add the fennel seeds, tinned tomatoes and the basil stalks. Bring to a simmer and let bubble away for 15 minutes.

4. Cut the fennel into thin wedges and the courgette into long strips. Add to a bowl and toss with the remaining 2 tablespoons of olive oil while you preheat the grill. Arrange your courgettes and fennel across a few large baking trays, then grill until they take on some colour. Flip over and cook for another few minutes.

5. Add the ricotta to a bowl with the zest of the lemon and grate in half the Parmesan. Add plenty of salt and pepper and mix together.

6. Preheat the oven to 200°C/180°C fan/gas mark 6.

7. Grab a baking dish and spread a spoonful of the tomato sauce across the bottom. Layer up some of the grilled fennel and courgette and top with basil leaves and a layer of ricotta. Repeat until all the ingredients have been used.

8. Top with the breadcrumbs, grate over the remaining Parmesan and bake for 30–40 minutes until bubbling, golden brown and crispy.

9. Serve with a rocket salad and warm focaccia.

Paprika Pork *with Romesco,* **Chickpeas & Kale**

GF DF

This one's a little bit special. Paprika-spiced pork loin is roasted until it's mouthwateringly juicy and laid to rest on a bed of glossy, garlicky chickpeas and a smoked almond romesco sauce. We've used 2 tins of chickpeas, making this dish very high in fibre and protein. The key to getting a nice crust on your pork is getting your roasting tray super-hot before it goes in the oven.

Cook time: 45 mins

Ingredients

Serves 4

- 100g (3½oz) smoked almonds (or use salted and roasted almonds instead)
- 450g (1lb) jar of roasted peppers
- 2 tbsp olive oil, plus 2 tsp
- 2½ tsp smoked paprika
- 1–3 tbsp sherry vinegar (depending on how sharp you like it)
- 1 pork tenderloin fillet (about 500g/1lb 2oz)
- 6 garlic cloves
- 400g (14oz) cherry tomatoes
- 2 × 400g (14oz) tins of chickpeas
- 200g (7oz) kale
- a handful of parsley
- salt and black pepper

Make it Vegetarian: Simply replace the pork with 250g (9oz) halloumi. Cut into strips and fry in a little smoked paprika until crisp.

Ingredient Hack: If you want to go boujee, use a jar of giant chickpeas instead.

Method

1. Preheat the oven to 220°C/200°C fan/gas mark 7. Put a roasting tin (big enough to fit the whole pork tenderloin in) into the oven to heat up for 10 minutes – this is the secret to getting a nice crust.

2. Meanwhile, make the romesco. Put three-quarters of the smoked almonds into a blender or food processor along with 4 of the peppers, 1 tablespoon of the olive oil and ½ teaspoon of the smoked paprika and 2 tablespoons of water. Blitz to a chunky sauce. Season to taste with vinegar, salt and pepper. Set aside.

3. Using kitchen paper, pat the pork loin dry, then rub with 2 teaspoons of olive oil and sprinkle all over with salt, pepper and the remaining 2 teaspoons of smoked paprika. Carefully place into the hot roasting tin and roast for 20–30 minutes, turning halfway, until cooked through. To check it's done, slice into the centre – you want it to be very juicy and creamy white with just a touch of pink. (But if you prefer slightly more cooked, cook for the extra time.)

4. While the pork is roasting, thinly slice the garlic cloves. Get a large, high-sided frying pan over a medium heat. Pour in the remaining tablespoon of olive oil and scrape in the garlic. Cook until turning very slightly golden, then tip in the cherry tomatoes.

5. Stir, then leave to cook while you slice the remaining roasted peppers from the jar. Drain one tin of chickpeas through a sieve.

6. Add the peppers to the pan along with the drained chickpeas and the second tin of chickpeas with their water. Turn the heat to high and cook, stirring occasionally, until the tomatoes begin to burst. Add the kale and cook until wilted, then season to taste with sherry vinegar, salt and pepper. Keep warm.

7. Allow the pork to rest for a few minutes, then cut into four pieces. Roughly chop the remaining almonds and parsley.

8. Spread a big spoonful of romesco into the base of four bowls, spoon over the garlicky, tomatoey kale and chickpeas, then place a piece of pork on top. Scatter over the almonds and parsley to serve. What a treat.

SUMMERY

Grilled Chicken Burger *with Mojo* **Verde**

DF

We had to include a recipe for a burger, and this one in particular has summer written all over it. Chicken breasts are bashed and tenderized before cooking for the ultimate juiciness, then served with a bright avo, red pepper and pickled jalapeño salsa, and mojo verde.

You will need baking paper and a rolling pin.

Cook time: 40 mins

Ingredients

Serves 4

2 tsp cumin seeds
a large bunch of coriander
1 fat garlic clove
2 tsp sherry vinegar, plus a splash to taste
6–8 pickled jalapeños (depending on how spicy you like it), plus a splash of the pickling liquid
2 tbsp plus 2 tsp olive oil
2 ripe avocados
3 roasted red peppers from a jar
4 skinless and boneless chicken breasts
4 brioche burger buns
4 small handfuls of rocket
salt and black pepper
chips, to serve (optional)

Method

1. Toast the cumin seeds in a small dry frying pan over a medium heat until smelling amazing, then set aside to cool slightly.

2. Mojo verde time. Put three-quarters of the coriander (stalks and all) into a blender along with the garlic clove, sherry vinegar, half the pickled jalapeños and 1 tablespoon of the olive oil. Tip in the cumin seeds, pour in 2 tablespoons of water and blitz to a smooth green sauce, adding a splash more water if it needs loosening – you want it to be a thick, drizzle-able consistency. Season to taste and put in the fridge.

3. For the salsa, halve the avocados, remove the pits and cut into cubes, then tip into a bowl. Cube the peppers, chop the remaining coriander (stalks and all) and add these to the avocado. Finely chop the remaining jalapeños and stir into the salsa with another tablespoon of olive oil, then season with salt, pepper, a splash of sherry vinegar and the pickling liquid from the jalapeños to taste. Set aside.

4. Put two of the chicken breasts between two sheets of baking paper, a few centimetres apart from each other. Using a rolling pin, bash the chicken to tenderize and flatten it slightly to a thickness of about 2cm (¾in). Repeat with the remaining chicken breasts, then season them all with salt and pepper. Rub over the remaining 2 teaspoons of olive oil.

5. Get your largest griddle or non-stick frying pan searingly hot. Lay in the chicken breasts, cook for 4–5 minutes each side until the chicken is cooked through and juicy.

6. Cut the buns in half, lightly toast in the pan, then assemble your burgers. Spread the base of the buns with half the mojo verde sauce, then top with chicken, then avo salsa, then rocket. Drizzle over the remaining mojo verde and sandwich together to serve – with chips if you like. (Who wouldn't?)

Hidden *Veg* **Tagliatelle**

This is a lovely way to sneak a lot of veg into what looks like a simple tomato sauce. Thrown together with tagliatelle and finished with fresh tomatoes and creamy ricotta, it's summer on a plate.

Cook time: 35 mins

Ingredients

Serves 4

3 garlic cloves
1 onion
2 carrots
2 celery sticks
3 tbsp olive oil
2 × 400g (14oz) tins of chopped tomatoes
1 tsp salt
a small bunch of basil
400g (14oz) cherry tomatoes
½ lemon
320g (11¼oz) tagliatelle
160g (5¾oz) ricotta
salt and black pepper

Method

1. Peel the garlic and roughly chop the onion, carrots and celery. Add everything to a blender and whizz until the veg has become a paste.

2. Heat a large saucepan over a medium heat and add 2 tablespoons of the olive oil. Add the veg paste and cook gently for about 10 minutes, stirring occasionally, until it becomes golden brown and soft.

3. Add the tinned tomatoes and 1 teaspoon of salt and tear in three-quarters of the basil leaves. Allow to cook at a gentle simmer for 25 minutes.

4. Meanwhile, dice up the cherry tomatoes and mix in a bowl with the juice of half a lemon and the remaining tablespoon of olive oil. Set aside.

5. Bring a large saucepan of salted water to the boil. Cook the pasta until al dente, following the packet instructions, then drain, reserving a mug of pasta water.

6. Toss the pasta with the cooked sauce and a splash of the pasta cooking water until the pasta is well coated.

7. Spoon into four shallow bowls and top with a couple of spoonfuls of the fresh tomatoes and a spoonful of ricotta. Roughly chop and sprinkle over the remaining basil.

Fish Piccata *with Fennel* Salad

DF

We love the contrast between the delicacy of the fish in its caper-y white wine sauce and the crisp and lemony crunch of the fennel salad. Be sure to slice your fennel as thinly as you can. It makes all the difference to this ridiculously fresh recipe.

Cook time: 35 mins

Ingredients

Serves 4

60g (2¼oz) pine nuts
2 fennel bulbs
1½ lemons
4 tbsp olive oil
1 tsp smoked paprika, plus a pinch
2 handfuls of rocket
2 tbsp plain flour
4 thick skinless white fish fillets (we like hake or haddock)
a large glass of white wine
3 tbsp capers
a handful of parsley
salt and black pepper

Method

1. Toast the pine nuts in a small dry frying pan over a medium heat until golden – watch closely as they can suddenly turn.

2. Pick the green fronds off the fennel bulbs and tear into a large bowl, then very thinly slice the fennel and add this too. Finely grate in the zest of 1 lemon, then squeeze in the juice. Add 1 tablespoon of the olive oil and a pinch of smoked paprika and then use your hands to scrunch the fennel into the lemon juice – this will help it soften. Mix through the rocket and toasted pine nuts, then season the salad to taste and set aside.

3. Spoon the plain flour onto a plate and stir through the remaining 1 teaspoon of smoked paprika. Pat the fish fillets completely dry with kitchen paper, then season with salt and pepper and coat lightly on both sides in the flour mix.

4. Get a large non-stick frying pan over a medium–high heat. Pour 2 tablespoons of olive oil into the pan. When hot, lay in the flour-dusted fish and fry for 2 minutes on each side. Transfer the fish to a plate.

5. Put the pan back over a medium heat, add the last tablespoon of oil, then add the white wine and capers. Squeeze in the juice of the remaining lemon half. Bring the sauce to a simmer while you roughly chop the parsley (stalks and all).

6. Gently place the fish back into the pan and cook for a minute or so more, basting with the sauce, until warmed through. Scatter over the parsley, then serve straight from the pan, alongside the fennel and rocket salad, and pretend you're on holiday.

Grilled Peach *& Courgette* **Panzanella**

V

Peaches are a great and easy way to add nutrients to a salad. Making the most of summer produce, this recipe will prove to you that salads are anything but boring. We've got everything from crunchy croutons to a warm curry leaf dressing and burrata involved in this triumph. Enough said.

Cook time: 45 mins

Ingredients

Serves 4

1 small ciabatta
4 tsp sesame seeds
1 tbsp olive oil, plus 2 tsp
3 medium courgettes
1 lime
3 flat peaches (or use normal peaches instead)
2 large or 3 small balls of burrata
a handful of basil
a handful of mint
a handful of coriander
1 tsp chilli flakes
salt and black pepper

For the dressing

3 tbsp olive oil
4 cloves garlic
12 fresh curry leaves
a small bunch of basil
2 limes

Ingredient Hack: If you haven't got particularly juicy lemons, use two in the dressing instead.

Method

1. Preheat the oven to 200°C/180°C fan/gas mark 6.

2. Tear the ciabatta into croutons and toss onto a baking tray with 2 teaspoons of sesame seeds. Season, then evenly drizzle over 1 tablespoon of the olive oil. Roast in the oven for 10–12 minutes until deeply golden and crisp. Set aside.

3. Meanwhile, peel the courgettes into thin ribbons with a vegetable peeler. Put into a large bowl, add 2 teaspoons of olive oil, the zest and juice of the lime and some seasoning and toss to evenly coat. Core the peaches and cut into wedges. Halve the lime.

4. Tear a piece of baking paper the same size as the bottom of your griddle pan and place it in the pan (the paper stops the peaches from sticking to the pan). In batches, lay the peach wedges on top and season with salt and black pepper. Cook for 2 minutes on each side until caramelized and beginning to get jammy, then transfer to the bowl with the courgettes.

5. Dressing time. Add your olive oil to a frying pan over a medium heat and heat gently. Finely slice the garlic and add to the pan with the curry leaves. Cook until the garlic is lightly golden and the curry leaves have crisped up.

6. Remove the garlic and curry leaves from the pan with a slotted spoon, then leave on a plate to cool. Once your fragrant oil has cooled to room temperature, pour it into a food processor and add your basil leaves. Blend to an oil, then add the zest and juice of your limes. Season to taste with salt.

7. Tear the burrata over the courgette and peach salad, then dot over the croutons. Spoon over the banging fragrant dressing, and sprinkle over the crispy garlic and curry leaves, basil, mint and coriander. Sprinkle over the remaining sesame seeds and chilli flakes to serve.

Sesame-Crusted *Fish with* Tomato Salad

GF DF 30

We wanted a recipe that celebrated tomatoes at their best but also wanted one that wasn't the same old 'eat them raw with a pinch of salt and olive oil'. That's why we've opted for big flavours and showered those toms in fish sauce and lime juice. The perfect side to bring out the best of spice-coated fillets of fish.

Cook time: 25 mins

Ingredients

Serves 4

4 skin-on white fish fillets (we like hake or haddock)
3 tbsp sesame seeds
2 tsp chilli flakes
8 very ripe large tomatoes
7 tsp sesame oil
2 banana shalllots
3 garlic cloves
4 tbsp rapeseed oil
2 super juicy limes
2 tbsp fish sauce
1 tsp soft light brown sugar
a small bunch of Thai basil (or regular, if you can't find it)
a handful of mint
salt and black pepper
carbs and greens of your choice, to serve

Fancy Hack: If you can get a mix of black and white sesame seeds they will look amazing.

Method

1. Preheat the oven to 200°C/180°C fan/gas mark 6 and line a roasting tin with foil or baking paper. Remove the skin from the fish and mix the sesame seeds and chilli flakes together in a small bowl.

2. Slice the tomatoes into thin rounds and season with salt.

3. Lay the fish, skin-side down into the lined roasting tin. Season well with salt and pepper then rub 1 teaspoon of sesame oil across the top of each fillet. Once oiled, sprinkle over the spiced sesame seeds to crust. Roast in the oven for 8–10 minutes until the fish is just cooked and will flake easily.

4. Finely slice your shallots into rounds, and finely slice your garlic. Heat your oil over a low heat in a frying pan, then add your shallots. Cook for 5 minutes until they are just starting to change colour, then add your garlic. Fry for another couple of minutes until they are all lightly crispy and golden, then lift out with a slotted spoon and drain on a plate lined with kitchen paper.

5. While the fish is roasting, make the dressing. Squeeze the juice of the lime into a small bowl, add the remaining 3 teaspoons of sesame oil, the fish sauce and brown sugar. Stir together until the sugar dissolves. Pour any water that has come off the tomatoes into the dressing and season to taste – you want it to be nice and punchy.

6. Arrange the tomatoes over a platter or divide between four plates. Pour over the dressing and tear over the Thai basil and mint. Top with the fish and crispy shallots and garlic, then serve with carbs of your choice and any greens you like.

Chicken *Souvlaki* **Salad**

We've taken all of our favourite elements from a souvlaki wrap and turned it into a salad. Yes, you read that right. The secret here lies in the reverse marinade – a method where you plunge the chicken into a bath of lemony spices after it's fully cooked, giving it this incredibly luxurious dressing.

Cook time: 35 mins

Ingredients

Serves 4

3 white pitta breads
3 tbsp olive oil, plus 2 tsp
1 small red onion
2 lemons
1 tsp dried oregano
2 tsp smoked paprika
2 tsp ground cumin
2 tsp dried mint
500g (1lb 2oz) skinless chicken thigh fillets
1 cucumber
160g (5¾oz) Greek yoghurt
4 ripe tomatoes
½ iceberg lettuce
a small bunch each of mint and parsley
salt and black pepper

Method

1. Preheat the oven to 200°C/180°C fan/gas mark 6.

2. Using scissors, snip the pitta into triangles straight into a bowl. Season generously, then drizzle in 1 tablespoon of the olive oil, using your hands to coat the bread evenly. Tip out onto a large baking tray and spread into a single layer. Bake for 8–10 minutes until crisp. Set aside.

3. Finely slice the red onion and toss in the juice of half a lemon.

4. Meanwhile, in a large bowl, mix together 2 tablespoons of the olive oil with the dried oregano, smoked paprika, cumin and 1 teaspoon of the dried mint. Zest and juice in 1 lemon and season with salt and pepper. Set aside – you will marinate your chicken in this once it's cooked (the secret to extra flavour and juiciness).

5. Tear a large piece of baking paper onto the work surface. Lay half the chicken thighs on the paper, a few centimetres apart from each other, then top with another sheet of baking paper. Using a rolling pin satisfyingly bash the chicken to an even thickness, around 1cm (½in). Repeat until all the thighs are flattened, season and rub with the remaining 2 teaspoons of olive oil

6. Get a large griddle or frying pan searingly hot. Once hot, lay in the chicken and cook for 4–5 minutes on each side until cooked through and juicy. Transfer the hot chicken to the marinade bowl.

7. Tzatziki time. Coarsely grate half the cucumber and squeeze out as much water as you can. Put into to a bowl with the remaining 1 teaspoon of dried mint and the Greek yoghurt. Squeeze in the juice of the remaining lemon and season to taste.

8. Slice the rest of the cucumber into long diagonals, chop the tomatoes and shred the iceberg lettuce. Pick the mint leaves and roughly chop the parsley (stalks and all).

9. Assembly time. Slice the chicken and return to the marinade bowl. Divide the cucumber, red onion, tomato, lettuce and herbs between four plates. Scatter over the pitta chips, then top with the chicken, spooning over all the delicious marinade. Top with little dollops of tzatziki and grate over lemon zest to serve.

Rainbow *Chard* Risotto

V GF

Risotto just got fresher with the addition of rainbow chard – packed with vitamin C, iron and calcium. Chard is an underused green that's sits somewhere between spinach and kale in terms of its subtle earthy flavour. We've moved away from the classically beige risotto to one that's packed full of spiced tomatoes and garlicky goodness instead. And we've thrown in some marinated feta. It's phenomenal.

Cook time: 1 hr

Ingredients

Serves 4

150g (5½oz) feta
1 lemon
1 tbsp za'atar
2 tbsp olive oil
1 onion
4 fat garlic cloves
200g (7oz) rainbow chard
200g (7oz) arborio risotto rice
2 tbsp tomato purée
3 tbsp harissa (we like rose harissa)
400g (14oz) cherry tomatoes
1 large glass of white wine
1 litre (1¾ pints) hot vegetable or chicken stock
a handful of parsley leaves
salt and black pepper

Make it Vegetarian: Use vegetable instead of chicken stock.

Ingredient Hack: If you can't find chard, use spinach or kale instead

Gluten-Free: If you're cooking gluten-free, check the label of the stock.

Method

1. Break the feta into decent chunks into a small bowl. Zest over the lemon, sprinkle over the za'atar and add 1 tablespoon of the olive oil. Set aside to marinate.

2. Finely chop the onion and garlic. Thinly slice the chard stalks, leaving the leaves to one side for later.

3. Get a large high-sided frying pan over a medium heat. Pour in the remaining tablespoon of olive oil, then tip in the onion and chard stalks. Cook, stirring occasionally, until soft (about 8 minutes), then add the garlic and cook for 1 minute more.

4. Tip in the risotto rice, then add the tomato purée and harissa. Give everything a good stir to coat the rice in the harissa mix. Toast for a minute then add the cherry tomatoes and white wine.

5. Once the wine has bubbled away, pour in a decent glug of stock. Cook, stirring regularly until the stock has been absorbed by the rice, then add a glug more. Keep cooking in this way for about 20 minutes until most of the stock has been absorbed, the cherry tomatoes have burst and the rice is tender with a slight bite.

6. Roughly slice the chard leaves and stir into the risotto. Once wilted, season with salt, pepper and lemon juice to taste. If the risotto is a little thick, add some more stock – you want it to be a sloppy consistency.

7. Spoon into bowls, top with the feta and parsley and it's good to go.

Zingy Blood Orange *Ceviche* **Tostadas**

GF DF 30

Ceviche fans, we've got you. This recipe will have you lightly curing sea bass in orange, lime, ginger, coriander and garlic before serving on the crunchiest baked tortillas with creamy avo, fresh chilli and radish. Be sure to use the highest quality fish you can find.

Cook time: 20 mins

Ingredients

Serves 4

8 corn tortillas
2 tbsp olive oil, for brushing
3cm (1¼in) piece of fresh ginger
2 garlic cloves
4 blood oranges (or use normal oranges if these aren't available)
4 limes
3 sea bass fillets, skin removed and pin-boned
a bunch of coriander
2 avocados
1 red onion
1 fresh jalapeño
6 radishes
a big pinch of Aleppo pepper or dried chilli flakes
sea salt

Fresh Hack: Sea bass is both delicate and versatile, making it the perfect backdrop for these fresh and vibrant tostadas packed with blood oranges, which contain anthocyanins – powerful antioxidants.

Method

1. Preheat the oven to 200°C/180°C fan/gas mark 6.

2. Brush the tortillas with a little olive oil and place directly onto the shelves of the oven to toast. Flip occasionally until golden and crisp – this should take 6–7 minutes.

3. Meanwhile, crush the ginger and garlic with the back of a heavy knife and chuck them into a bowl. Add the juice of 3 of the blood oranges and 2 of the limes. Cut the fish into thin slices and add to the juice mixture. Rip the stalks from the coriander and chuck those into the bowl too. Season generously with salt and set aside for 20 minutes.

4. Halve the avocados and remove the pits, then scoop the flesh into a blender with the juice of 1 lime and a big pinch of salt. Whizz until smooth.

5. Thinly slice the red onion, jalapeño and radishes, then peel and cut the remaining blood orange into segments – cut the peel off the orange, trimming away any excess pith. Cut along the inside lines of each segment to release them.

6. Once the fish has had 20 minutes in the juice, spread a spoon of the avocado onto each tostada and top with a generous spoonful of the ceviche.

7. Scatter with the red onion, jalapeño, radishes and coriander leaves and finish with a big pinch of Aleppo pepper. Serve with the remaining lime, cut into wedges for squeezing.

Slow-Roasted *Tomato & Halloumi* **Couscous**

V

This one is all about the dressing. Half the slow-roasted tomatoes are blitzed up with garlic, chilli and basil to make a chunky, rustic sauce that you'll want to pour on literally everything. We've put it to good use here by tossing it with giant couscous, olives and crunchy halloumi croutons.

Cook time: 55 mins

Ingredients

Serves 4

800g (1lb 12oz) cherry tomatoes
5 garlic cloves (unpeeled)
3 tbsp olive oil
200g (7oz) kale
1 tsp smoked paprika
150g (5½oz) Kalamata olives
250g (9oz) wholewheat giant couscous
1 lemon
½–1 red chilli (depending on how spicy you like it)
a small bunch of basil
250g (9oz) pack of halloumi
salt and black pepper

Method

1. Preheat the oven to 160°C/140°C fan/gas mark 3.

2. Take the cherry tomatoes off the vine and put them and the garlic cloves onto a large baking tray in a single layer. Season with salt and pepper and drizzle over 1½ tablespoons of the olive oil, then roast for 35–40 minutes until the garlic is completely soft and the tomatoes are shrivelled, sweet and on the edge of bursting.

3. Tip half the kale onto a large baking tray, toss with the smoked paprika, ½ tablespoon of oil and some seasoning, then spread into an even layer so that it roasts evenly. Put on the shelf below the tomatoes and roast for 10–12 minutes, flipping halfway until crisp.

4. Meanwhile, pit the olives, if needed, and cook the giant couscous according to the packet instructions.

5. Tip the remaining kale into your largest bowl, tear up any larger leaves and chop any thick stems, then zest and squeeze in the juice of the lemon. Season well, then use your hands to scrunch the kale into the lemon – this will help it soften.

6. Dressing time. Squeeze the cooked garlic cloves out of their skins into a blender. Roughly chop the red chilli (seeds and all) and cut the basil stalks away from the leaves (saving the leaves for later). Put the chilli and basil stalks into the blender along with the garlic. Add half the roasted tomatoes, along with any roasting juices from the tray and the remaining tablespoon of olive oil, then blitz to an unreal dressing. Season to taste.

7. Drain the couscous, rinse under cold water until cool, then shake off any excess water. Tip into the bowl with the kale and add the pitted olives. Tear in the remaining basil leaves, pour in most of the dressing and give everything a good toss to combine.

8. Cut the halloumi into small cubes, then get a non-stick frying pan over a medium–high heat. Add the halloumi and fry until deeply golden, about 2 minutes on each side.

9. Divide the tomatoey-kale couscous between four plates, drizzle over the remaining dressing and top with the remaining roasted tomatoes, fried halloumi and crispy kale. Yes please.

Curried Chickpea *& Mango* Salad

VG DF

Tossed with crispy spiced chickpeas, zesty coconut yoghurt and tamarind, this recipe takes the flavours of chaat and throws them into a summery salad. Chickpeas are a great healthy source of protein and fibre. A wonderful side dish that proves how diced mango can make pretty much anything refreshing.

Cook time: 40 mins

Ingredients

Serves 4

2 × 400g (14oz) tins of chickpeas
1 tsp garam masala
½ tsp chilli powder
1 tbsp olive oil
1 ripe mango
2 ripe avocados
2 wholemeal chapatis
a bunch of mint
2 red chillies
200g (7oz) coconut yoghurt
2 limes
4 tbsp tamarind sauce
salt and black pepper

Make it Vegan: Check the label on the chapatis.

Method

1. Preheat the oven to 200°C/180°C fan/gas mark 6.

2. Drain the chickpeas from their liquid into a sieve. Tip them into a large roasting tin and sprinkle over the garam masala, chilli powder, a good pinch of salt and the olive oil. Toss in the tray to combine, then roast in the oven for 20 minutes.

3. Meanwhile, peel and dice the mango and avocados into 1cm (½in) chunks.

4. Get the roasting tin out of the oven and tear in the chapatis. Return to the oven for another 10 minutes, tossing halfway through to ensure they cook evenly.

5. Meanwhile, finely chop the mint leaves and red chillies and set a tablespoon of each aside for later. Tip the coconut yoghurt into a bowl, then add the bulk of your chillies and mint to it, along with the juice from 1 of the limes. Mix to combine, then season to taste.

6. Toss the crispy chickpeas and chapatis with the diced mango and avocado. Transfer to a serving dish, then spoon over the green coconut yoghurt and tamarind sauce. Sprinkle with your reserved mint and chillies, then serve with the remaining lime, cut into wedges for squeezing over.

Prawn Summer Bowls *with Nước Chấm* **Dressing**

GF DF 30

Think of this fresh and vibrant prawn salad packed with fresh herbs and nutrient-dense raw veg as a bit like a deconstructed summer roll. It's the perfect thing to take on a picnic and devour on a hot and sunny day.

Cook time: 20 mins

Ingredients

Serves 4

2 garlic cloves
2 red chillies
4 tbsp fish sauce
50g (1¾oz) caster sugar
1 lime
2 carrots
1 cucumber
a handful each of coriander and mint
400g (14oz) vermicelli rice noodles
150g (5½oz) beansprouts
300g (10½oz) cooked prawns
10 prawn crackers

Ingredient Hack: Switch out the prawns for any leftover cooked protein, or even crispy tofu.

Method

1. To make the nước chấm dressing, finely chop the garlic and chillies and add to a small bowl with the fish sauce, caster sugar and juice of the lime. Add 4 tablespoons of boiling water and combine until the sugar is dissolved and the sauce is smooth.

2. Julienne or coarsley grate the carrots and cut the cucumber into half moons. Chop the coriander (stalks and all) and the mint.

3. Cook the vermicelli rice noodles according to the packet instructions.

4. Pile the noodles into a large serving bowl and top with the carrots, cucumber, beansprouts, coriander and mint.

5. Top with the cooked prawns, crumble in the prawn crackers and pour over the nước chấm dressing. Toss together and serve immediately.

Courgette *& Ricotta* **Galette**

V

You can use this simple galette recipe in so many ways. We've added hazelnuts to the pastry for an extra healthy source of fat. This summery version is made with courgettes but it's a great vehicle for any good seasonal veggies (or fruits). Don't be afraid to get creative.

Cook time: 1 hr + chilling

Ingredients

Serves 4

You will need cling film and baking paper

For the pastry

75g (2¾oz) hazelnuts
250g (9oz) plain flour, plus a little extra for dusting
125g (4½oz) cold butter
1 medium egg

For the filling and herby dressing

2 courgettes
200g (7oz) ricotta
30g (1oz) Parmesan (or vegetarian alternative)
15g (½oz) basil
15g (½oz) mint
1 lemon
3 tbsp olive oil
salt and black pepper

Method

1. Start with the pastry. Blitz the nuts in a food processor until finely chopped. Add the flour and a pinch of salt and whizz again until combined.

2. Cut the butter into roughly 2cm (¾in) cubes and add to the flour. Pulse until the mixture resembles breadcrumbs. Add the egg and 2 tablespoons of cold water and mix again until the mixture starts to come together. Tip out onto a work surface and knead gently, just to bring the pastry together. Shape into a disc, wrap in cling film and chill for an hour, or overnight.

3. To make the filling, slice the courgettes into roughly ½cm (¼in) thick rounds. Toss with a generous pinch of salt and place into a colander for 20 minutes to drain out the excess moisture.

4. Add the ricotta to a large bowl and finely grate in the Parmesan, then finely chop and add half of the basil and mint and the zest of the lemon, a big pinch of salt and grind of black pepper. Mix to combine.

5. Preheat the oven to 200°C/180°C fan/gas mark 6 and line your largest baking tray with baking paper.

6. Remove the pastry from the fridge and place onto a floured work surface. Dust the pastry in flour and roll out into a circle roughly 30cm (12in) in diameter and ½cm (¼in) thick. Slide the pastry onto the lined baking tray.

7. Spread the base with the ricotta mix, leaving a 6–7cm (2¼in–2¾in) gap around the edges. Pat the courgettes dry with kitchen paper, then arrange over the base in concentric circles. Fold the edges of the pastry over, crimping as you go to make the borders.

8. Bake in the centre of the oven for 30 minutes until the pastry is golden brown.

9. Meanwhile, finely chop the remaining herbs and mix in a small bowl with the olive oil, a pinch of salt and the juice of the lemon.

10. Remove the galette from the oven, drizzle over the herby oil and allow to rest for 5 minutes before serving.

mob

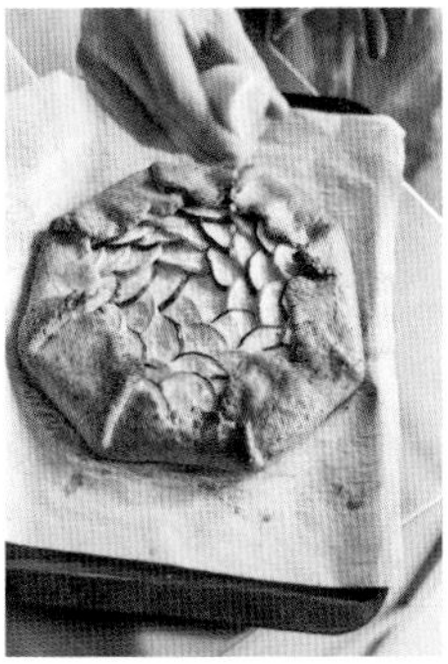

Lebanese Moussaka *with Greek Yoghurt* **& Toasted Pine Nuts**

V GF

Easily our most-loved food creation: the contrast between the soft, rich aubergine and the tangy Greek yoghurt makes this recipe restorative, gut-friendly and satisfying without being too heavy.

Cook time: 55 mins

Ingredients

Serves 4

For the aubergine

2 large aubergines
4 tsp olive oil
½ tsp each of ground cumin, chilli powder, ground cinnamon

For the moussaka

1 onion
6 garlic cloves
1 tbsp olive oil
1 tsp each of ground cumin and cinnamon
½ tsp chilli powder
2 tbsp tomato purée
1 × 400g (14oz) tin of chickpeas
600g (1lb 5oz) vine tomatoes
300ml (10½fl oz) vegetable stock
1½ tbsp pomegranate molasses
½ tbsp dried mint
40g (1½oz) pine nuts
8 tbsp Greek yoghurt
salt
toasted pitta bread, to serve

Make it Vegan: Swap the yoghurt for rice or use a non-dairy alternative.

Gluten-Free: Serve with rice instead of pitta bread and check the label of your stock.

Ingredient Hack: If you don't have pomegranate molasses, you can substitute with brown sugar.

Method

1. Preheat the oven to 200°C/180°C fan/gas mark 6.

2. Prep your aubergines by cutting into thick cubes about 2cm (¾in) in length.

3. Tip the aubergines into a roasting tin, add the olive oil and spices, and season with salt and combine with your hands. Roast in the oven for 10 minutes, then give them a good stir and roast for a further 15 minutes until softened and caramelized but not 100 per cent cooked through – they will finish cooking in the moussaka sauce. Set aside, then turn off the oven.

4. Finely chop the onion and thinly slice the garlic. Pour the olive oil into a large saucepan with a lid, add the chopped onion and cook over a medium heat until really soft, about 8 minutes.

5. Add the garlic to the pan and cook for 2 minutes more.

6. Increase the heat to medium–high, add the cumin, cinnamon, chilli powder and tomato purée. Drain the chickpeas and add these too. Cook for about 5 minutes, stirring regularly, until lightly browned.

7. Quarter the tomatoes and stir into the pan. Add the stock, pomegranate molasses, dried mint and a pinch of salt. Cook for 10 minutes over a medium heat with the lid on.

8. After 10 minutes, add the roasted aubergine cubes and simmer for a further 8–10 minutes with the lid on.

9. Meanwhile, toast the pine nuts in a small frying pan over a medium heat until nicely toasted.

10. Remove the moussaka from the heat and let it cool slightly. Add a generous spoonful of Greek yoghurt to each plate, then spoon over the moussaka. Finish with a sprinkle of toasted pine nuts and serve with warm pitta bread.

SHARING

Charred Aubergine Salad *with Pomegranate* **& Tomatoes**

VG V GF

We've taken all the elements of a baba ghanoush and turned it into a pitta-scooping sharing feast by topping that much-loved smoky dip with spicy caramelized nuts and a bright pomegranate and tomato salad. A real hands-on way to eat.

Cook time: 1 hr

Ingredients

Serves 4

3 large aubergines
60g (2¼oz) mixed nuts
1½ tsp ground cumin
1½ tsp smoked paprika
1 tsp honey or maple syrup
3 tbsp tahini
1 lemon
200g (7oz) mixed baby tomatoes (we like the mix of colours; you can also use cherry tomatoes instead)
4 spring onions
80g (2¾oz) pomegranate seeds
2 tbsp pomegranate molasses
2 tbsp olive oil
a large handful of dill
salt and black pepper
toasted pitta bread, to serve

Make it Vegan: Use maple syrup instead of honey.

Gluten-free: Serve with gluten-free bread.

Method

1. You're going to cook the aubergine directly over the flames of a gas hob. If you don't have one, preheat the grill to high.

2. Put the aubergines either directly over the flame, or under the grill. Cook, turning occasionally, until the outside is completely blackened and the aubergines have collapsed. This will take longer under the grill, be patient.

3. Once the aubergines are cooked, transfer to a bowl and leave to cool slightly – they will soften even more in the bowl.

4. Meanwhile, preheat the oven to 180°C/160°C fan/gas mark 4. Line a small roasting tin with baking paper. Tip in the mixed nuts, toss with 1 teaspoon each of ground cumin and smoked paprika and season with salt and pepper. Roast in the oven for 6–8 minutes until lightly golden, then drizzle over the honey or maple syrup and return to the oven for 2 minutes until nicely caramelized. Leave to cool.

5. Come back to the aubergines. Drain away any water from the bottom of the bowl, then peel away as much blackened skin from each aubergine as you can and discard – don't worry about there being a little left, it will just add to the flavour. Once peeled, roughly mash the aubergine back in the bowl with a fork. Stir in the tahini and remaining ½ teaspoon each of cumin and smoked paprika, then season with salt, pepper and lemon juice to taste. Set aside.

6. Tomato time. Quarter the tomatoes and add to another bowl. Thinly slice the spring onions (both green and white parts) and add these too along with the pomegranate seeds, pomegranate molasses and olive oil. Roughly chop the dill, add most to the bowl, stir and season to taste, adding any remaining lemon juice if you want to.

7. Roughly chop the cooled nuts. Spoon the aubergine onto the bottom of a platter, top with the pomegranate and tomato salad, then scatter over the spiced nuts and remaining dill. Serve with toasted pitta bread for scooping.

Spiced Lamb Koftas with *Watermelon, Feta* & Pickled Chilli

GF

This is the ideal dish to cook when you've got people over and you don't want to spend your entire day hiding in the kitchen. The koftas come together quick as a flash and the meaty lamb paired with the sweet watermelon, salty feta and tangy heat of the pickled chillies bangs.

Cook time: 30 mins

Ingredients

Serves 4

50g (1¾oz) mixed seeds
2 tbsp shawarma seasoning (or Lebanese seven-spice), plus 1 tsp
500g (1lb 2oz) lamb mince
4 tsp olive oil
1 small watermelon (sometimes called baby watermelon in the supermarket)
8 pickled green chilli peppers, plus 2 tbsp pickling liquid
120g (4¼oz) feta
a small bunch of mint
1 tsp sumac
salt and black pepper

Serving Hack: Feeding a crowd? Pair this with our charred aubergine salad with pomegranate & tomatoes and flatbreads (see previous page) for the ultimate sharing feast.

Method

1. Toast the seeds in a dry frying pan over a medium heat until beginning to pop, then remove from the heat and stir through 1 teaspoon of the shawarma seasoning. Season, then set aside to cool.

2. Tip the lamb mince into a large bowl and spoon in the remaining 2 tablespoons of shawarma seasoning along with plenty of salt and pepper. Using your hands, scrunch the flavourings into the meat, then shape the lamb mince into 12 oval koftas, each around 2.5cm (1in) long.

3. Get your largest frying or griddle pan searingly hot. Rub 2 teaspoons of oil over the koftas then place into the pan. Fry for 5–6 minutes on each side until the meat is cooked through, juicy and tender – don't be tempted to flip them too early otherwise they will stick to the pan.

4. Meanwhile, peel the watermelon and cut into wedges. Divide between four plates or stick on a large platter for people to share. Thinly slice the chillies on the diagonal, scatter over the top of the watermelon, then crumble over the feta in decent chunks.

5. Once the koftas are cooked, pour the remaining 2 teaspoons of oil over the watermelon salad along with the 2 tablespoons of pickling liquid. Season with loads of black pepper, then tear over the mint leaves and scatter over the spiced seeds. Serve the watermelon salad and kofta together to set the perfect summer scene, sprinkled with sumac on top.

Spatchcocked *Chicken with* **Herby Rice Salad**

GF DF

This is what you'll want to make when your mates are round: juicy, golden roast chicken topped with a zingy tomato and olive salsa, served with a herb-packed caramelized onion and rice salad. All of it, of course, gets even better when doused in those glorious chicken juices.

Cook time: 1 hr

Ingredients

Serves 4

1 garlic bulb
1.2kg (2lb 10oz) whole chicken
2 tbsp olive oil
2 onions
250g (9oz) brown rice
60g (2¼oz) pine nuts
a small bunch each of mint and parsley
100g (3½oz) mixed olives
200g (7oz) cherry tomatoes
2 tbsp sherry vinegar
½ tsp smoked paprika
50g (1¾oz) sultanas
salt and black pepper

Method

1. Preheat the oven to 220°C/200°C fan/gas mark 7.

2. Slice the top off the garlic bulb and plonk into the centre of a large roasting tin. Lay the chicken, breast-side down, onto a chopping board with its legs towards you, then using sharp scissors, cut down either side of the backbone to remove it. Now place the chicken, breast-side up, on top of the garlic, then use your hands to flatten the meat. Season all over with salt and pepper, then rub the skin with 1 tablespoon of the olive oil. Roast in the oven for 40 minutes until super golden and the juices run clear when you cut into the thickest part of the thigh.

3. Meanwhile, thinly slice the onions and tip into a medium saucepan placed over a medium-heat. Pour in 250ml (9fl oz) water and a pinch of salt and cook for about 20 minutes until all the water has evaporated, then turn up the heat to medium-high, add the remaining tablespoon of olive oil and cook, stirring regularly, for 10 minutes until golden and caramelized.

4. While the onions are cooking, cook the brown rice according to the packet instructions. Toast the pine nuts in a small dry frying pan over a medium heat until golden – watch closely as they can suddenly turn. Roughly chop the mint leaves and all the parsley (stalks and all).

5. Salsa time. Scrape a third of the chopped herbs into a small bowl. Roughly chop the olives and tomatoes and add them to the bowl along with the vinegar and smoked paprika. Season to taste – you want it fresh and zingy.

6. Once the chicken is cooked, leave it to rest for 15 minutes while you finish the rice. Tip the cooked rice into a serving bowl – if any of the rice is clumping together, rinse it through a sieve and shake off any excess water first. Get the garlic out from under the chicken, mash with a fork, then stir through the rice. Mix through the caramelized onions, toasted pine nuts, sultanas and remaining herbs. Pour any of the resting chicken juices through the rice salad (hello!) and season to taste.

7. Carve the chicken onto a platter, spoon over the olive salsa and serve with the rice salad for people to help themselves.

Chickpea & *Sweet Potato Curry* **with Sambol**

VG GF DF

If you are craving a hearty midweek dinner packed with veg, this fragrant curry is the one for you. The coconut sambol is a Sri Lankan condiment often used to top curries, lending a wonderful freshness.

Cook time: 1 hour

Ingredients

Serves 4

2 sweet potatoes
2 tbsp coconut oil
2 tbsp mild curry powder
2 red onions
6 garlic cloves
4cm (1½in) piece of fresh ginger
1 red chilli
4 medium tomatoes
1 tsp cumin seeds
½ tsp black mustard seeds
½ tsp ground turmeric
1 cinnamon stick
1 tsp chilli powder
200ml (7fl oz) coconut milk
1 × 400g (14oz) tin of chickpeas
handful of coriander leaves
salt

For the coconut sambol

65g (2½oz) desiccated coconut
1 lime
1 tsp chilli powder
a bunch of coriander

Method

1. Preheat the oven to 200°C/180°C fan/gas mark 6.

2. Peel and chop the sweet potatoes into medium-sized chunks. Toss them in a roasting tin along with a good pinch of salt, 1 tablespoon of the coconut oil and 1 tablespoon of the curry powder. Roast for 45 minutes until cooked through and slightly charred.

3. Meanwhile, thinly slice the onions and finely chop the garlic, ginger and red chilli. Whizz up your tomatoes in a blender, or roughly chop them.

4. Add 1 tablespoon of the coconut oil to a large saucepan and allow to melt over a medium heat. Add the cumin seeds and mustard seeds and cook for 1 minute until they start to pop. Tip the sliced onion into the pan and fry for 15 minutes until soft.

5. Add your chopped garlic, ginger and chillies, along with the turmeric, remaining tablespoon of curry powder, cinnamon stick and chilli powder. Cook, stirring, for 2 minutes.

6. Tip the blitzed tomatoes into the pan and cook for 5 minutes until reduced. Add the coconut milk and chickpeas, then simmer for 15 minutes until reduced.

7. To make the sambol, soak your desiccated coconut in cold water for 15 minutes, then squeeze out the excess liquid. Add the zest and juice of your lime, your chilli powder and a pinch of salt. Get a dry frying pan over medium heat, then toast your coconut mixture for 3 minutes until fragrant and lightly golden.

8. Add the roasted sweet potato to the curry and simmer for 5 minutes. Season to taste with salt, then spoon into bowls and serve topped with the coconut sambol and coriander leaves.

Mob's Mezze **Board**

V

There's nothing more satisfying than good bread and good dips. We've pickled some veg to keep things lively here and paired them with a tahini-laden hummus, a vibrant pink beetroot yoghurt that is an easy way to add plenty of nutrients, and a smoky spiced matbucha. A proper spread.

Cook time: 30 mins

Ingredients

Serves 4

250g (9oz) cooked beetroot
100g (3½oz) Greek yoghurt
1 small garlic clove
1 tsp dried mint
1 × 400g (14oz) tin of chickpeas
3 tbsp tahini
1 tsp ground cumin
1 lemon
1 tsp sumac
2 roasted red peppers from a jar
3 large ripe tomatoes
2 tsp smoked paprika
1 tsp chilli flakes
2 tbsp olive oil, plus extra to serve
salt and black pepper
flatbreads, to serve

For the quick-pickled vegetables

½ cucumber
2 medium carrots
a small handful of dill
2 tsp coriander seeds
3 tbsp white wine vinegar
1 tsp caster sugar
a good pinch of salt

Method

1. First make the quick-pickled vegetables. Slice the cucumber and carrots into thin rounds and roughly chop the dill. Toast the coriander seeds in a dry frying pan over a medium heat until smelling amazing, then tip into a large bowl Add the carrot and cucumber, then pour over the vinegar and add the sugar and salt. Mix everything together to combine and leave to pickle for 10–15 minutes.

2. For the beetroot yoghurt dip, drain the liquid away from the cooked beet, roughly chop them, then add to a blender or food processor with the Greek yoghurt, garlic and dried mint. Blitz until smooth. Season to taste and put into a small bowl.

3. Next up, hummus. Wash the food processor/blender then drain the chickpeas over a bowl, keeping the liquid. Tip the chickpeas into the blender, adding enough chickpea liquid to get your desired consistency. Add the tahini and ground cumin and squeeze in the juice of half the lemon. Blitz until velvety, season to taste, then spoon into a separate bowl and sprinkle with the sumac.

4. Last up the matbucha; this one's a winner. Chop the roasted red peppers and tomatoes and add to a small bowl with the smoked paprika, chilli flakes, olive oil and remaining lemon juice. Season to taste.

5. Serve the mezze with warmed flatbreads and the quick-pickled veggies. It's all about those dips.

Spiced Roast Chicken *with Fennel, Orange* **& Lime Pickle Slaw**

GF

This super-juicy, lightly spiced chicken is perfect stuffed into a flatbread with a handful of lively fennel slaw. We think a crunchy citrus slaw is the perfect way to inject some tasty goodness to this dish – raw vegetables and citrus have a higher vitamin content due to the availability of water-soluble nutrients such as vitamin C and B vitamins, all of which can be lost when cooked. Feel free to sub in mango chutney if lime pickle isn't for you.

Cook time: 1 hr 30 mins + marinating

Ingredients

Serves 4

1 tsp black pepper
2 tsp cumin seeds
1 tsp coriander seeds
250g (9oz) natural yoghurt
3 garlic cloves
30g (1oz) piece of fresh ginger
3 tsp medium curry powder
1.4kg (3lb) free-range chicken
2 fennel bulbs
1 orange
a bunch of mint
1 lemon
1 tbsp lime pickle
salt
flatbreads, to serve

Gluten-free: Serve with gluten-free flatbread and check the label of your curry powder.

Method

1. Toast the pepper, 1 teaspoon of the cumin seeds and the coriander seeds in a dry pan over a medium heat until fragrant.

2. Coarsely grind the spices in a pestle and mortar, then add to a bowl with the yoghurt.

3. Grate in the garlic and ginger and add the curry powder and a generous whack of salt.

4. Season the chicken generously with salt and rub with the marinade, both outside the chicken and inside the crevices, then cover and pop in the fridge for 8–12 hours.

5. When you are ready to cook, preheat the oven to 180°C/160°C fan/gas mark 4.

6. Place the chicken into a roasting tin and chuck into the oven for 1 hour 15 minutes–1 hour 20 minutes until the juices run clear when you cut into the thickest part of the thigh.

7. While the chicken is cooking, make your slaw. Thinly slice the fennel and chuck into a bowl.

8. Toast the remaining teaspoon of cumin seeds and add to the fennel. Peel and segment the orange and add to the bowl along with any extra juice. Tear in the mint and add a squeeze of lemon juice.

9. When the chicken is cooked, allow it to rest for 15 minutes before carving into pieces. Serve with big handfuls of slaw, a dollop of pickle and flatbreads.

Turmeric Lamb *with Tamarind* **Chickpeas**

GF

This showstopper involves a bit of simple butchery for helping up your skillset. Rubbing the lamb in yoghurt and spices balances out the richness of the meat, especially when it's served with a sharp chickpea and potato salad and some coriander chutney. Leg of lamb can be quite a fatty meat, so we've reduced the amount of oil used.

Cook time: 1 hr 30 mins + marinating

Ingredients

Serves 4

½ leg of lamb (about 1.2kg/2lb 10oz)
thumb-sized piece of fresh ginger
2 limes
180g (6½oz) Greek yoghurt
2 tsp ground turmeric
500g (1lb 2oz) new potatoes
1 tbsp cumin seeds
1 tbsp olive oil, plus 1 tsp
a large bunch of coriander
2 tbsp desiccated coconut
1–2 green chillies (depending on how spicy you like it)
1 × 400g (14oz) tin of chickpeas
1 red onion
1 lemon
300g (10½oz) cherry tomatoes
a bunch of mint
4 tbsp pomegranate seeds
2 tbsp tamarind paste
salt and black pepper

Cooking Hack: This lamb would also be great cooked on the barbecue in summer – roast the potatoes in the oven while you barbecue and rest the meat.

Method

1. The day before, place the lamb leg, meatier-side down, onto a chopping board. Cut down vertically along the length of the bone. Keep cutting the meat away, keeping as close to the bone as possible until you can remove it. Open out the meat, cutting into any thick pieces, until you have a flat joint of the same thickness.

2. Squash the lamb into a large bowl and season generously with salt and pepper. Finely grate in the ginger, zest and juice of 1 of the limes, and dollop in 150g (5½oz) of the the yoghurt and the turmeric. Rub the marinade into the lamb (get into all the crevices), then cover and chill for at least 4 hours or overnight.

3. Preheat the oven to 200°C/180°C fan/gas mark 6. Bring the lamb to room temperature. Halve the new potatoes, toss in a bowl with the cumin seeds, seasoning and 1 tablespoon of the olive oil.

4. Spread the lamb out into your largest roasting tin. Add the potatoes, then drizzle over the remaining olive oil. Roast for 25–35 minutes, depending on how thinly you butterflied it.

5. Meanwhile, make the chutney. Put most of the coriander into a blender with the coconut and half the green chilli. Add the juice of the remaining lime, 3 tablespoons of water and blitz to a textured sauce, adding a little more water if too thick. Season to taste.

6. Come back to the lamb. Once cooked, transfer to a chopping board, cover with foil and leave to rest. Drain and rinse the chickpeas through a sieve, then tip into the roasting tin and mix into the potatoes and lamb juices. Return to the oven for 15–20 minutes until the potatoes are cooked through.

7. Meanwhile, thinly slice the red onion and squeeze over the juice of the lemon to lightly pickle them. Thinly slice the remaining chilli. Roughly chop the tomatoes, remaining coriander (stalks and all) and mint leaves. Scrape everything into the tin with the cooked potatoes and chickpeas, add the pomegranate seeds and tamarind paste. Toss to combine and season to taste.

8. Thinly slice the lamb or serve whole at the table for people to carve themselves, with the remaining yoghurt to drizzle over. Plonk everything on the table and begin feasting.

Honey Roasted Roots *with Feta and* Yoghurt

V GF

We all know roasting root veg is a game-changer. But just you wait until you've tried them caramelized with honey and spices, draped on a bed of creamy yoghurt. Take care to cut the beetroot and carrot into the same size here so they roast evenly. Beetroot is a wonderful source of dietary fibre and helps increase blood flow to the brain; that's why we've used plenty of it in this recipe.

Cook time: 45 mins

Ingredients

Serves 4

1kg (2lb 4oz) carrots
500g (1lb 2oz) beetroot
3 tbsp olive oil
1½ tbsp cumin or coriander seeds (your choice)
1 tbsp smoked paprika
1 lemon
170g (6oz) Greek yoghurt
1 tbsp honey
a handful each of parsley, dill and mint leaves
75g (2¾oz) feta
a handful of pickled chillies
salt and black pepper
flatbreads, to serve

Gluten-free: Serve with gluten-free flatbread.

Method

1. Preheat the oven to 220°C/200°C fan/gas mark 7.

2. Peel the carrots and beetroot, then cut into similar-sized smallish chunks. Tip into your largest roasting tin (or two tins if that's easier), toss with the olive oil, cumin or coriander seeds, smoked paprika and plenty of seasoning, then spread out into a single layer so that they cook evenly. Roast for 25 minutes.

3. Finely grate the zest of the lemon into the yoghurt. Mix together, then season with salt, pepper and lemon juice to taste.

4. Come back to the roots: flip them over and drizzle over the honey. Roast for a further 5–10 minutes until sticky, tender and caramelized. Meanwhile, roughly chop the parsley and dill and tear the mint leaves.

5. Spoon the yoghurt into the centre of a serving dish. Pile on the roasted roots, making sure to scrape all the goodness from the tray as well. Crumble over the feta and scatter over some pickled chillies and the herbs. Serve with flatbreads for dunking or, if you prefer, assemble into an epic wrap.

Dukkah Lamb Steaks *with Charred* **Baby Gem**

GF DF

Homemade dukkah is rich in vitamins, minerals and fibre. Here it adds a spiced nutty crunch to the grilled lamb steaks in this Middle Eastern-inspired recipe, while the harissa and honey dressing take a simple charred lettuce salad to the next level. Elegant and deceptively easy to make.

Cook time: 45 mins

Ingredients

Serves 4

- 50g (1¾oz) hazelnuts (use blanched if you can find them)
- 3 tbsp sunflower seeds (or use mixed seeds)
- 1 tbsp cumin seeds
- 1 tbsp coriander seeds
- 4 roasted red peppers from a jar
- 2–3 tbsp harissa (depending on how spicy you like it)
- 2 tsp honey
- 2 tbsp olive oil, plus 4 tsp
- 1 lemon
- 4 baby gem lettuces
- 4 lamb steaks
- a small handful of mint
- salt and black pepper

Cooking Hack: The lamb and baby gem would be great cooked on the barbecue!

Method

1. Roughly chop the hazelnuts. Toast in a dry frying pan over a medium heat until just golden, then tip into a small bowl. Toast the sunflower seeds in the same pan until beginning to pop and add to the hazelnuts. Finally, toast the cumin and coriander seeds until smelling amazing, then take the pan off the heat and leave to cool slightly.

2. Once cooled, grind the cumin and coriander seeds, then stir them through the hazelnut and seed bowl. Season with a little salt. Get in – you've just made dukkah! (To crust the lamb with later.)

3. Dressing time. Finely chop the red peppers and add to a small bowl along with the harissa, honey and 2 tablespoons of olive oil. Zest and juice in the lemon, stir together and season to taste. Set aside.

4. Get your largest frying pan over a high heat and wait until it is searing hot – this will take a couple of minutes. Meanwhile, cut the baby gem lettuces in half.

5. Rub the 4 teaspoons of olive oil over the lamb steaks and season well with salt and pepper. Add the steaks to the hot pan and cook for 2½–3 minutes on each side until cooked to your liking. Once the lamb steaks are cooked, tip half the dukkah onto a large plate and place the lamb on top, then pat over the remaining dukkah and leave to rest.

6. Keep the pan over a high heat and lay the baby gem in, cut-side down. Fry for a minute or so until the underside is blackened and the lettuce has started to soften, then transfer to four plates and spoon over the harissa pepper dressing. Tear over the mint leaves.

7. Slice the steaks and serve alongside the charred baby gem salad, scraping over any of the crusted juices. A real win.

Roasted *Celeriac with* **Muhammara**

VG GF DF

Muhammara is a delicious sweet and spicy dip from Syria – this version of the recipe comes courtesy of a close friend, Jana. It's perfect alongside the nutty roasted celeriac and with a zingy, herby salad that elevates this dish nutritionally.

Cook time: 2 hrs 45 mins

Ingredients

Serves 4

1 large celeriac
4 tbsp olive oil, plus extra for drizzling
100g (3½oz) walnuts
1 garlic clove
450g (1lb) jarred roasted red peppers
1 tbsp Aleppo pepper or chilli flakes
4 tbsp pomegranate molasses
1 lemon
1 red onion
a small bunch each of mint, parsley and coriander
salt and black pepper

Method

1. Preheat the oven to 200°C/180°C fan/gas mark 6.

2. Trim the celeriac to get rid of the roots and scrub thoroughly to remove any dirt. Rub all over with ½ tablespoon of the olive oil and a generous pinch of salt, then wrap well in foil. Place into the oven and roast for 2–2½ hours, or until a knife can be easily inserted through the centre.

3. Meanwhile, make the muhammara. Add the walnuts to a food processor and blitz until they resemble breadcrumbs. Grate in the garlic, then drain and add the peppers, the Aleppo pepper, 2 tablespoons of the pomegranate molasses, the juice of half the lemon, ½ teaspoon of salt and 1 tablespoon of olive oil. Blitz until you have a fairly smooth and creamy sauce. Taste and add more lemon juice or salt if needed.

4. To make the salad, thinly slice the red onion and roughly chop all of the herbs. Mix in a bowl along with the juice of the other lemon half, 1½ tablespoons of olive oil, 1 tablespoon of pomegranate molasses and a pinch of salt.

5. Once the celeriac is ready, remove from the oven and take off the foil. Heat a frying pan over a medium-high heat and add the remaining 1 tablespoon of olive oil.

6. Slice the celeriac into 2cm (¾in) thick slices and fry for 2 minutes on each side until it turns golden brown.

7. Spread 3 tablespoons of the muhammara onto each plate, top with the celeriac slices and drizzle over the remaining pomegranate molasses and a little olive oil. Serve with the herby salad alongside.

Hot Sauce *Prawns with* **Coleslaw**

GF DF

We first saw the idea for charred coleslaw on a programme about Southern American barbecue. Charring the cabbage without cooking it beforehand adds a clever smoky depth that complements the honey and hot sauce-glazed prawns. The perfect sweet-and-spicy situation

Cook time: 35 mins

Ingredients

Serves 4

1 small white cabbage
a bunch of spring onions
2 tsp Dijon mustard
2–3 tbsp apple cider vinegar
3 tbsp olive oil
2 tsp honey
3 medium carrots
a small bunch of parsley
3 tbsp hot sauce (we like Frank's or Cholula)
800g (1lb 12oz) raw shell-on king prawns
salt and black pepper

Ingredient Hack: If you can't find fresh shell-on king prawns, buy frozen ones and defrost them thoroughly – pat dry with kitchen paper before using.

Cooking Hack: The prawns and coleslaw would be great cooked on a barbecue!

Method

1. Get your largest frying pan over a high heat. You want it searingly hot, to char the vegetables without cooking them all the way through. While the pan is heating, cut the cabbage lengthways into quarters.

2. Lay the cabbage into the pan, cut-side down. Cook until the underside is blackened, then turn to the second side and char that too – you're looking to char and just soften the cabbage a little. Transfer to a chopping board.

3. Next, lay the whole spring onions into the pan. Cook for about a minute or so on each side until they too are blackened and then transfer to the chopping board. Take the pan off the heat.

4. While the veg is cooling, make the dressing. Spoon the mustard, vinegar, olive oil and 1 teaspoon of the honey into a large bowl. Stir to combine.

5. Coarsely grate the carrots into the dressing bowl, then, using a sharp knife, thinly slice both the cabbage and spring onions and scrape these in too. Roughly chop the parsley (stalks and all), add to the dressing, then give everything a good toss to combine, using your hands to massage the dressing into the slaw. Season to taste and set aside.

6. Prawn time. Mix the remaining teaspoon of honey with the hot sauce and 2 tablespoons of warm water. Stir until the honey dissolves.

7. Put the pan back over a searingly high heat (no need to wash in between!) – you want it almost smoking. Season the prawns, then add to the pan – you may need to do this in two batches. Cook for 2–3 minutes until the prawns have all turned completely pink and have charred slightly. If you've cooked in batches, add all the prawns back to the pan, then pour in the hot sauce glaze.

8. Cook, tossing the prawns in the glaze for 30 seconds more, then tip into a serving bowl.

9. Serve the prawns and the coleslaw in the middle of the table for people to help themselves. (Kitchen paper may be needed!)

mob

STAUB
STAUB

Root Veg *Tabbouleh with* **Green Harissa**

VG DF

Love harissa? Wait until you've tried this. Make your own micronutrient-filled green harissa dressing while the rest of your tabbouleh is coming together for the freshest salad around.

Cook time: 50 mins

Ingredients

Serves 4

150g (5½oz) pearled spelt or pearl barley
1 garlic bulb
2 green peppers
a bunch of spring onions
1–2 green chillies (depending on how hot you like it)
1 small butternut squash
1 small celeriac
3 tbsp olive oil
4 tsp cumin seeds
4 tsp coriander seeds
2 tbsp mixed seeds
a large bunch each of coriander and parsley
2 lemons
200g (7oz) radishes
80g (2¾oz) pomegranate seeds
salt and black pepper

Ingredient Hack: Make sure you taste your green chillies before roasting – if they are extra hot you will only need one.

Cooking Hack: For a real smoky depth to your harissa you can always char the peppers, garlic, chilli and spring onions in a griddle pan instead. Roasting them in the oven along with the root vegetables is just the most hassle-free option.

Method

1. Preheat the oven to 220°C/200°C fan/gas mark 7.

2. Cook the spelt or barley according to the packet instructions.

3. Slice the top off the garlic bulb, then put it into a roasting tin along with the whole green peppers, whole spring onions and green chillies. Roast for 30 minutes until the veg is soft and charring.

4. Meanwhile, prep your root veg. Peel the butternut and celeriac, then cut both into similar-sized wedges. Tip into your largest roasting tin, toss with 2 tablespoons of the olive oil and plenty of seasoning, then spread into a roughly single layer, so that they roast evenly. Put on the shelf underneath the green vegetables and roast for 25–30 minutes, flipping halfway until tender and caramelized.

5. Meanwhile, toast the cumin and coriander seeds in a dry frying pan over a medium heat until smelling amazing. Tip three-quarters of the toasted seeds into a blender and tip the rest into a bowl.

6. Put the pan back over a medium heat. Add the mixed seeds and toast until they begin to pop, then pour into the bowl with the cumin and coriander seeds. Stir together, season and set aside.

7. Green harissa time. The green veg should now be charred. Once cool enough to handle, deseed the peppers and put into the blender with the seeds, along with the whole spring onions. Cut the stalks off the chillies and add these too, then squeeze in the roasted garlic. Tip in the toasted seeds, then add most of the coriander and parsley (stalks and all). Pour in the final tablespoon of olive oil, then zest and squeeze in the juice of both lemons. Blitz to a smooth green drizzle-able sauce. Season to taste.

8. Drain and rinse the cooked spelt or barley through a sieve, shake off any excess water and tip into a large serving bowl.

9. Quarter the radishes and add to the serving bowl along with most of the pomegranate seeds and all of the roasted root veg. Roughly chop the remaining herbs (stalks and all). Add these too, then pour in most of the green harissa dressing. Carefully fold everything together.

10. Season to taste, then drizzle over the remaining green harissa, scatter over the seeds and remaining pomegranate seeds and serve.

PUDDINGS

Creamy *Coconut Rice* **Pudding**

VG GF DF

Nothing says comfort like a good rice pud; we've made this version vegan by cooking it in a little brown sugar and coconut milk. Using coconut milk is a delicious and genius way to make this rice pudding super-creamy without being too heavy. Find the ripest mango you can for the topping to give it some real tropical vibes.

Cook time: 35 mins

Ingredients

Serves 4

200g (7oz) pudding rice
50g (1¾oz) soft light brown sugar
a pinch of salt
2 × 400ml (14fl oz) tins of coconut milk
2 tbsp coconut flakes
2 tbsp shelled pistachios
1 ripe mango
1 lime
2 tbsp maple syrup

Method

1. Measure the rice, sugar and salt into a large saucepan. Tip in the coconut milk, plus a tin of water, then cook over a medium heat, stirring often so that it doesn't catch or bubble over, for about 30 minutes until the rice is cooked and creamy with a slight bite.

2. Meanwhile, toast the coconut flakes in a dry fying pan over a medium heat, just until lightly browned. Remove from the pan and then roughly chop the pistachios.

3. Once the rice pudding is nearly cooked, turn down the heat to low while you peel and dice the mango. Spoon the rice pudding into four bowls, top with the diced mango, coconut flakes and pistachios and then zest over the lime and drizzle over the maple syrup. Comfort pud at its best.

Clementine, Almond *& Olive Oil* **Cake**

(V) (GF) (DF)

This is the cake that keeps on giving. It seems to get more delicious over time and only gets better after a few days in a tin. That's largely thanks to its cushiony texture and the sweet and zesty flavour it gets from blitzing whole clementines (skin and all). We used olive oil instead of butter as it's rich in nutrients and a healthy source of fat.

Cook time: 1 hr 35 mins

Ingredients

Serves 8–10

You will need baking paper, a 20cm (8in) cake tin (preferably springform) and a skewer or cocktail stick

5 clementines (sometimes called easy peelers in the supermarket)
120ml (4fl oz) olive oil, plus a little for greasing
4 medium eggs
200g (7oz) caster sugar
200g (7oz) ground almonds
2 tsp baking powder
a pinch of salt
4 tbsp icing sugar
Greek yoghurt, to serve

Dairy-Free: Serve with coconut yoghurt instead of Greek yoghurt.

Gluten-Free: Check the label on the baking powder.

Utensil Hack: Don't have a skewer or cocktail stick? Use a piece of dried spaghetti instead to check that the cake is done.

Method

1. Get a saucepan of water on to boil. Once boiling, add 3 of the clementines and boil until completely soft – this will take about 30 minutes. Drain and leave to cool slightly.

2. Preheat the oven to 180°C/160°C fan/gas mark 3. Grease a 20cm (8in) cake tin all over with a little oil and line the base with baking paper.

3. Cut the cooked clementines in half and remove any visible pips, then put the clementines, skin and all, into a food processor. Blitz to a smoothish paste – this will make your whole kitchen smell unreal.

4. Next, crack the eggs into a large bowl. Measure in 150g (5½oz) of the sugar and whisk well (a hand whisk is fine here) until the mixture lightens in colour – this will take a couple of minutes – then whisk in the olive oil. Scrape in the clementine paste, whisk again to combine, then fold in the ground almonds and baking powder along with a decent pinch of salt.

5. Pour the cake batter into the lined tin. Bake for 45–50 minutes until deeply golden and cooked through – prod a skewer or cocktail stick into the centre of the cake to check it's done; it should come out clean with a few crumbs attached.

6. While the cake is baking, make the syrup. Measure the remaining 50g (1¾oz) of sugar along with 3 tablespoons of water into a small saucepan. Put over a low heat and leave to cook gently until the sugar has dissolved. Once the sugar has dissolved, turn up the heat to medium, bubble away until you have a thick syrup, then take off the heat and squeeze in the juice of the remaining 2 clementines. Leave to cool.

7. Poke holes using the skewer or cocktail stick all across the top of the warm baked cake. Drizzle over the syrup, then leave the cake to cool completely in its tin. Once cool transfer to a plate, dust over the icing sugar, cut into slices and serve with Greek yoghurt.

8. This cake will keep well for up to 3 days in an airtight container, though some even say it improves with age!

Berry & Chocolate *Ganache* **Tart**

It's hard to believe but this super-rich and indulgent chocolate tart is made with water, not cream. We'd bet good money that this will become your new favourite pudding.

Cook time: 1 hr + chilling

Ingredients

Makes 12

You will need baking paper, a 20cm (8in) loose-bottomed tart tin and baking beans or rice.

150g (5½oz) cold butter
200g (7oz) plain flour, plus a little for dusting
2 tbsp cocoa powder
5 tbsp icing sugar
300g (10½oz) dark chocolate
1 tsp vanilla extract
400g (14oz) berries of your choice (we like strawberries and raspberries)
1 tbsp booze of your choice (optional – we like rum or whisky)
sea salt

Ingredient Hack: Wrap any leftover pastry tightly in cling film and freeze for another time.

Cooking Hacks: If you're running short of time, chill the lined pastry case in the freezer until hard, instead of in the fridge.

Make the chocolate tart the day before, then macerate the berries before serving.

Method

1. First make the pastry. Cut 125g (4½oz) of the butter into small cubes. Put into a food processor along with the flour, cocoa powder, 3 tablespoons of the icing sugar and a good pinch of salt. Blitz until it resembles clumpy breadcrumbs, then add 2 tablespoons of cold water and pulse again until the pastry is just coming together. Tip out onto your surface and briefly knead until smooth. Wrap in cling film and chill in the fridge for 30 minutes.

2. Remove the chilled pastry from the fridge and dust your work surface with flour. Roll out the pastry to roughly ½cm (¼in) thickness and use to line a 20cm (8in) tart tin. Press the pastry into the edges of the tin – don't worry if there is a little bit of pastry overhanging the edges. Prick the base of the pastry with a fork and put back into the fridge, uncovered, to chill for 20 minutes.

3. Preheat the oven to 180°C/160°C fan/gas mark 4.

4. Tear a sheet of baking paper large enough to completely cover the tart tin, then scrunch into a ball. Smooth out and place inside the tin, over the pastry. Tip in enough baking beans or rice so that you fill the tart tin, then put into the oven to bake for 15 minutes. This is called blind baking.

5. After 15 minutes use a spoon to carefully remove the baking beans or rice (save these, they can be reused endlessly!), then remove the paper and slide the empty pastry case back into the oven for 3–5 minutes until cooked through. Leave to cool completely. Once the pastry is cold, trim off any excess pastry using a serrated knife, then make your ganache.

6. Finely chop the chocolate and tip into a large bowl. Add the vanilla, the remaining 25g (1oz) butter and a big pinch of sea salt, then pour over 200ml (7fl oz) boiling water. Leave for a minute so the chocolate begins to melt, then whisk to a smooth ganache – trust us, this actually works.

7. Pour the ganache into the pastry case. Put into the fridge, uncovered, to set – this will take about 2 hours.

8. Once the tart is nearly set, slice any larger berries and then tip them all into a large bowl. Add the remaining 2 tablespoons of icing sugar and the booze, if using. Toss together so that the berries get coated in the sugar. Set aside to macerate (a fancy word for softening and creating their own syrup).

9. To serve, take the chocolate tart out of its tin and put onto a serving plate. Top with the berries and all their juices and serve, somewhat smugly, at the middle of the table. This will keep for 2 days in the fridge.

Banana Ice Cream *with Chocolate* Hazelnut Sauce

VG GF DF

Trust us when we say that this healthy 'ice cream' is going to blow your mind – and that's not just because it's made by blitzing up frozen bananas. Using bananas to make the ice cream adds plenty of fibre and nutrients such as vitamin B6. We've gone one step further by adding a homemade hazelnut chocolate sauce. We're good to you like that.

Cook time: 30 mins + chilling

Ingredients

Serves 4

5 large bananas
50g (1¾oz) blanched hazelnuts
75g (2¾oz) dark chocolate
2–3 tsp maple syrup, to taste
a big pinch of sea salt

Vegan/Dairy-Free: Make sure your chocolate is dairy-free.

Method

1. The day before you want to eat this, peel and slice the bananas. Put into an airtight container or freezer bag and pop into the freezer until frozen solid.

2. When ready to eat, preheat the oven to 180°C/160°C fan/gas mark 4.

3. Tip the hazelnuts onto a baking tray. Toast in the oven for 6–8 minutes until golden, then leave to cool slightly.

4. Sauce time. Once the hazelnuts are cooled, tip most of them into a food processor. Blitz until very finely chopped and beginning to clump together – almost at a nut butter stage. Snap the chocolate into a heatproof bowl and melt, either in the microwave in 30-second bursts or over a pan of barely simmering water. Once melted, scrape into the processor. Add the maple syrup, 3 tablespoons of water and a big pinch of sea salt. Blitz again to a chocolate sauce; if you prefer it looser, stir in a splash more water. Scrape into a bowl.

5. Clean the food processor, then tip in the frozen bananas. Blitz until the texture of ice cream – trust us, be patient, this really works. If your processor is small, do this in two batches.

6. Roughly chop the remaining hazelnuts.

7. Divide the banana 'ice cream' between four bowls. Spoon over the chocolate sauce and served topped with the chopped hazelnuts.

Roasted Rhubarb *with Yoghurt* **& Sweet Dukkah**

V GF 30

When forced rhubarb is in season between January and March, you've got to make the most of it. Roasting it with orange, cardamom and honey offsets its natural tartness wonderfully. We've then topped it with a seeded pistachio dukkah for a good dose of protein and healthy fats, with a hint of coriander to really knock your socks off.

Cook time: 25 mins

Ingredients

Serves 4

1 orange
6 green cardamom pods
2 tbsp honey
400g (14oz) rhubarb
30g (1oz) shelled pistachios
1 tsp coriander seeds (optional)
2 tbsp sesame seeds
2 tbsp poppy seeds
a good pinch of sea salt
Greek yoghurt, to serve

Ingredient Hack: The sweet dukkah can be used on any yoghurt or fruit combo. Treat it like granola.

Method

1. Preheat the oven to 200°C/180°C fan/gas mark 6.

2. Zest and juice the orange into a large bowl. Using a pestle and mortar, lightly bash the cardamom pods to release the seeds, add the seeds to the bowl and stir in the honey. Cut the rhubarb into 2.5cm (1in) pieces, tip into the bowl and toss in the orange mixture, making sure each piece gets nicely coated.

3. Lay the rhubarb in neat rows, flat-side down, in a medium baking dish. Pour over the orange syrup. Roast in the oven for 20 minutes until the rhubarb is soft and just holding its shape.

4. Meanwhile, make the sweet dukkah. Roughly chop the pistachios and toast in a small dry frying pan over a medium heat until smelling toasty. Tip into a small bowl, put the pan back over the heat and toast the coriander seeds, if using, until smelling amazing. Add them to the pistachio bowl. Finally, toast the sesame seeds until just golden and scrape these into the bowl too. Leave to cool a little, then add the poppy seeds and sea salt.

5. To serve, spoon yoghurt into the bottom of each bowl and top with the rhubarb, a drizzle of the cooking syrup and the sweet dukkah. Equally as delicious for breakfast as for dessert.

Salted Honey *& Yoghurt* Cheesecake

(V) (GF)

This is a lighter version of the cheesecake you might already be familiar with: it's rich thanks to a combo of soft ricotta, tangy yoghurt and honey but it doesn't come with any of the baggage or heaviness of cream. Start with all your ingredients at room temperature for the best results.

Cook time: 3 hrs

Ingredients

Serves 8

You will need a 15cm (6in) springform tin and baking paper.

250g (9oz) thick Greek yoghurt
500g (1lb 2oz) ricotta
150g (5½oz) runny honey
3 eggs
1 tsp vanilla extract
1 orange
1 tsp sea salt
2 tbsp shelled pistachios

Method

1. Line a sieve with a clean tea towel and set it over a bowl. Add the yoghurt and ricotta to the lined sieve, then leave to strain for a couple of hours at room temperature.

2. Preheat the oven to 180°C/160°C fan/gas mark 4 and line a 15cm (6in) springform tin with two squares of baking paper.

3. Tip the ricotta and yoghurt into a large bowl, discarding any of the liquid that has come out of it, and whisk until smooth.

4. Add all but a tablespoon of the honey and whisk again. Add the eggs one at a time, whisking until you have a totally smooth batter before adding the next one. Add the vanilla extract, the zest of the orange and the sea salt, then whisk until just combined.

5. Pour the cheesecake mixture into the lined tin and bake in the middle of the oven for 45 minutes. When it is done, it should be set around the edges but jiggle in the middle.

6. Leave to cool to room temperature, then pop your cheesecake into the fridge to chill for a couple of hours.

7. When ready to serve, finely chop the pistachios. Remove the cheesecake from the tin and top with the remaining honey and chopped pistachios.

WÜSTHOF CLASSIC
Made in Solingen/Germany/2018

Baked Peaches *with Amaretti* Crumble

V GF 30

Peach, honey, and almond is an ultimate summer combo, and this easiest-ever crumble is sure to give you big holiday vibes whenever you eat it. We swapped sugar for honey in this recipe for its added health benefits and antioxidant properties. Make sure to use the ripest peaches you can get; the juicier the better.

Cook time: 25 mins

Ingredients

Serves 4

50g (1¾oz) butter
2 tbsp honey
75g (2¾oz) amaretti biscuits (approx. 6 biscuits)
3 tbsp flaked almonds
3 cardamom pods
4 ripe peaches
natural yoghurt
1 lime

Cooking Hack: If your peaches are underripe, cover the dish in foil once the crumble has browned and bake for an extra 5 minutes.

Method

1. Preheat the oven to 180°C/160°C fan/gas mark 4.

2. Melt the butter in the microwave or in a small saucepan. Once melted, stir in the honey, then crumble in the amaretti biscuits and add the flaked almonds. Bash the cardamom pods and remove the black seeds within. Finely chop them, then add to the saucepan. Mix the crumble topping together.

3. Halve and de-stone the peaches, then place them, cut-side up, into a baking dish. Fill/pile up each peach evenly with the crumble mixture, then bake for 20 minutes until the peaches are softened and the crumble deep golden.

4. Place a good dollop of yoghurt in each bowl and zest over the lime. Divide the crumble between the bowls, spooning over any juices from the peach dish, and serve for the speediest cheat's summer crumble vibes.

Plum *& Walnut* **Strudel**

(V)

Everything you like about a crumble encased in buttery, crispy, flaky filo. We love the plum, honey and cinnamon combo with the toasted walnuts teeing things off nicely and providing healthy fats, which are good for the heart. It's sublime.

Cook time: 1 hr + cooling

Ingredients

Serves 6

4 large or 6 smaller plums
1 tsp ground cinnamon
2 tbsp honey
1 lemon
50g (1¾oz) walnuts
1 tsp cornflour
50g (1¾oz) butter
6 sheets of filo pastry
1 tbsp icing sugar
ice cream, to serve

Method

1. Cut the plums in half, remove their stones, then slice into thick wedges. Put into a saucepan along with the cinnamon and honey, then zest and juice in the lemon. Cook over a medium heat, stirring occasionally, for about 10 minutes until the plums have softened but are just holding their shape – don't worry if a couple of the smaller wedges have broken down.

2. Meanwhile, roughly chop the walnuts and toast in a dry frying pan over a medium heat until lightly golden. Set aside.

3. Once the plums are softened, drain through a sieve into a large bowl to collect all of the cooking juices. Pour the juices back into the saucepan and tip the plums into the bowl. Mix the cornflour with 1 tablespoon of water in a small bowl until you have a smooth jelly-like sauce. Pour this into the saucepan, put over a medium–high heat and bubble away for a few minutes until you're left with a thick sauce. Leave to cool slightly, then pour over the plums. Add the walnuts, fold together and leave to cool completely. (You could even make this filling the day before.)

4. Once your filling is cold, preheat the oven to 180°C/160°C fan/gas mark 4. Line your largest baking tray with baking paper.

5. Melt the butter in the microwave or in a small saucepan. Unravel a sheet of filo pastry with one of the longer sides towards you, keeping the remaining pastry underneath a damp tea towel – this will stop it from drying out.

6. Brush the pastry liberally with melted butter, then lay a second sheet of filo, long side towards you, overlapping the first sheet by half. Brush it with melted butter then repeat, placing the third filo sheet over the first, and the second over the fourth and so on, brushing each with butter as you go.

7. Leaving a 5cm (2in) border of pastry facing towards you, spoon the cold filling along the length of the filo, then fold in the sides and carefully roll the pastry tightly away from you, to encase the filling into a long strudel cylinder.

8. Transfer the strudel to the lined baking tray (you may need to lie it diagonally) and brush with the remaining melted butter. Bake in the oven for 18–20 minutes until the pastry is deeply golden brown. Once baked, leave to cool for 10 minutes (an agonizing wait), then sift over the icing sugar. Cut into six using a serrated knife and serve with ice cream.

Chocolate *Mousse with* **Peanut Brittle**

V GF

We've gone proper homely with the base for this chocolate mousse, using eggs to aerate and lighten it up, so forgive us for getting a little fancy at the end by adding in a crunchy-meets-salty peanut brittle. It really does make all the difference.

Cook time: 25 mins + chilling

Ingredients

Serves 4

3 medium eggs
100g (3½oz) dark chocolate
5 tbsp caster sugar
30g (1oz) roasted salted peanuts
sea salt, for sprinkling
4 tbsp Greek yoghurt, to serve

Method

1. For the chocolate mousse, get out two large bowls. Separate the eggs, putting the yolks in one bowl and the whites in the second.

2. Snap the chocolate into a third heatproof bowl. Melt either in the microwave in 30-second bursts or over a pan of barely simmering water. Set aside to cool slightly.

3. Using an electric whisk, whisk the egg whites until they are super-white and fluffy and hold their shape once done. Without cleaning the beaters, add 2 tablespoons of caster sugar to the egg yolks and whisk together until pale and doubled in size.

4. Pour the melted chocolate into the egg yolks and briefly whisk to combine, then using a metal spoon or spatula, gently and efficiently fold the egg whites into the chocolate mixture – keep as much air as possible. Start by adding a large spoonful of egg white to loosen the chocolate mixture, then carefully fold in the rest.

5. Spoon the chocolate mousse into four small glasses, mugs or ramekins, then put in the fridge to chill for at least 2 hours.

6. Brittle time. Roughly chop the peanuts. Line a small baking tray with baking paper. Pack the peanuts into a compact rectangle in the centre of the tray. Spoon the remaining 3 tablespoons of sugar into a small frying pan over a medium heat. Without stirring (just swirling the pan instead), melt the sugar until it becomes an amber caramel, then immediately pour over the peanuts and leave to cool.

7. To serve, spoon a tablespoon of yoghurt over each mousse, then snap the peanut brittle into pieces and place these on top. Finish with a little sprinkle of sea salt. Unreal.

Carrot Cake with *Tahini* **Frosting**

V

Everyone loves a carrot cake, and it's only right that we've got a brilliant recipe for one in this book, made with honey instead of the sugar in the frosting and oil instead of butter in the batter. Ours is baked into a brownie tin for the perfect sheet cake look, then topped with the most ridiculously tasty cream cheese and tahini frosting. It is – quite simply – irresistible.

Cook time: 1 hr 15 mins

Ingredients

Serves 12

You will need baking paper, a 20cm (8in) square brownie tin (preferably springform) and a skewer or cocktail stick

100g (3½oz) walnuts
250g (9oz) carrots
250g (9oz) self-raising flour
½ tsp bicarbonate of soda
1½ tsp ground cinnamon, plus extra for sprinkling
1½ tsp ground ginger
a pinch of salt, plus extra for sprinkling
4 medium eggs
200g (7oz) soft light brown sugar
1 orange
200ml (7fl oz) vegetable oil, plus extra for greasing
salt

For the frosting

250g (9oz) cream cheese
3 tbsp honey
3 tbsp tahini
1 tsp vanilla extract

Utensil Hack: Don't have a skewer or cocktail stick? Use a piece of dried spaghetti to check that the cake is done instead.

Method

1. Preheat the oven to 180°C/160°C fan/gas mark 4. Grease a 20cm (8in) brownie tin or high-sided small roasting tray with oil and line the base with baking paper.

2. Tip the walnuts out onto a baking tray and toast in the oven for 6–8 minutes until nicely toasted. Leave to cool, then roughly chop.

3. Coarsely grate the carrots. Measure the flour, bicarb, cinnamon, ground ginger and salt together in a bowl.

4. Crack the eggs into a separate large bowl, add the sugar and zest in the orange. Using an electric whisk, whisk until the mixture is light and fluffy – it will almost treble in size. While still whisking, slowly pour in the oil.

5. Once all the oil has been incorporated, add the dry ingredients. Briefly whisk until you have a smooth batter, then fold through all the grated carrots and most of the chopped walnuts.

6. Spoon the cake batter into your lined tin and smooth out the top. Bake for 40 minutes until the cake is deep golden, risen and cooked through – prod a skewer or cocktail stick into the centre of the cake to check it is done – it should come out clean with a few crumbs attached. Leave to cool completely.

7. Once the cake is cool, make the frosting. Whisk all the ingredients together with 2 tablespoons of water until smooth.

8. Get the cake out of its tin, spread the frosting all over the top, then scatter over the remaining walnuts, plus a sprinkling of salt and cinnamon. Cut into 12 to serve. The cake will keep well in an airtight container for up to 3 days.

Miso & Peanut *Banana* **Split**

V GF 30

Caramelized bananas deserve a comeback – especially when they're cooked in an easy miso caramel with peanut butter yoghurt and pretzels, like they are in this recipe. We added miso to this dish, which not only tastes amazing but is fermented and so is good for your gut. This is the ultimate, feel-good speed pud.

Cook time: 15 mins

Ingredients

Serves 4

- 2–3 tsp miso (depending on how much oomph you want)
- 3 tbsp soft light brown sugar
- 2 tbsp peanut butter
- 4 small bananas
- 300g (10½oz) natural yoghurt
- 30g (1oz) salted pretzels or roasted and salted peanuts

Method

1. Using a fork, whisk the miso with 4 tablespoons of water in a small bowl until smoothish.

2. Get a large frying pan over a low heat. Spoon in the sugar then pour in the miso water. Leave to gently cook, without stirring (swirl the pan instead), until the sugar has dissolved into the water and begun to caramelize.

3. Meanwhile, stir the peanut butter with 2–3 tablespoons of warm water in a small bowl to loosen slightly. Cut the bananas in half lengthways.

4. Once you've got a caramel going, lay the bananas into the pan, cut-side down. Turn up the heat to medium and leave to cook away for a few minutes until the caramel clings to the bananas.

5. Assembly time. Spoon the yoghurt into the base of four small plates, spoon over the peanut butter, then top each plate with 2 halves of caramelized banana. Crumble over the pretzels or scatter over the peanuts, to serve. Seriously good.

Beetroot & *Stem Ginger* **Brownies**

V

These are the iconic Mob brownies that you already know and love with a secret veg surprise that has somehow made even fudgier . . .

Cook time: 50 mins

Ingredients

Makes 16

You will need baking paper and a 20cm (8in) square brownie tin (preferably springform).

250g (9oz) cooked beetroot
4 stem ginger balls, plus 2 tbsp stem ginger syrup
250g (9oz) dark chocolate
200g (7oz) butter, plus extra for greasing
200g (7oz) caster sugar
3 medium eggs
50g (1¾oz) self-raising flour
50g (1¾oz) cocoa powder
sea salt

For the stem ginger syrup

50g (1¾oz) caster sugar
4 tbsp stem ginger syrup
30g (1oz) butter
60ml (2fl oz) double cream

Method

1. Preheat the oven to 180°C/160°C fan/gas mark 4. Grease a 20cm (8in) brownie tin or high-sided small roasting tin with butter and line the base and sides with baking paper.

2. Drain the cooked beetroot, roughly chop and put into a food processor. Blitz until it is a thick purée consistency, then set aside. Roughly chop the stem ginger and 50g (1¾oz) of the dark chocolate and set that aside too.

3. Snap the remaining dark chocolate into a heatproof bowl and add the butter and a pinch of sea salt. Melt either in the microwave in 30-second bursts or over a pan of barely simmering water.

4. Next, tip the sugar into a large bowl and crack in the eggs. Using an electric whisk, whisk the eggs and sugar together until they have doubled in size and are very light and fluffy. Add the chocolate mixture, beetroot purée, stem ginger syrup, flour and cocoa powder. Whisk briefly until you have a rich combined batter.

5. Pour half the batter into your lined tin, dot with half the stem ginger and chocolate pieces, then spread over the remaining batter. Smooth out the top and dot with the remaining stem ginger and chocolate.

6. Sprinkle over a little sea salt, then bake for 25 minutes until the edges are set and the centre still has a good wobble.

7. Make your stem ginger syrup. Add your sugar, stem ginger syrup and butter to a saucepan. Cook down for 5 minutes to a dark brown bubbly sauce, then remove from the heat. Pour in your double cream and whisk to combine. Allow to cool to room temperature.

8. Drizzle your syrup on top of your brownies, leave to cool then cut into 16 squares. The brownies will keep well in an airtight container for up to 3 days.

Index

Acknowledgements

I have so many people I need to thank! This is our biggest and best book to date, and that is all down to the amazing team of people behind its production.

First and foremost, I would like to thank Sophie Godwin, who was behind most of the recipes in this book. You have created some incredible dishes for Fresh Mob and I can't wait for people to try them out.

A massive thanks also to the incredible Mob Food Team, all of whom have recipes throughout the various chapters. Sophie Wyburd, Jordon King, Seema Pankhania, Xiengni Zhou and Ben Lippett, thank you all. You are the beating heart of the Mob platform. A particular thanks to Sophie W, who oversaw the project internally. I am so grateful for all your work on this, and on everything else. Thank you.

And a huge thank you to the brilliant Lucy Sommer who worked as the nutritionist on the book. Thank you so much for all your advice and guidance throughout this process, and for making sure the recipes are as healthy-ish as possible!

On to the art direction and the styling – Ellie Silcock. You had a vision for this book, and the way it will look, and it is beautiful. You oversaw the whole thing, and I feel incredibly grateful to have been working side by side with someone so brilliant.

Next up, I would like to thank the master that is David Loftus. Best photographer I have ever worked with. It is a complete pleasure working with you, each and every time, and I am always blown away by the end result. Thank you again for taking us into your home for the last couple of days of the shoot, and again thank you to the ever-wonderful Ange for having us all.

A massive thanks also to Jodie Nixon, who was the Food Assistant on the book. Jodie, it is amazing the number of dishes you were getting through each day, thank you so much for all your work.

Thank you also to Charlie Phillips with the best props.

The design of the books is something I care about deeply. It is incredibly important to me that they look and feel beautiful. The designs for Fresh Mob were created by Studio Nari and Emma Dragovic. Thank you both for all the creativity you put into this project. The book looks stunning and it is all down to you.

Without our brilliant publisher, there would be no book, and so I'd love to thank the whole Hodder team. Carolyn Thorne, as ever you have been such a supportive, guiding presence throughout the project, and I am so grateful for the faith and trust you have had in me. And Issy Gonzalez-Prendergast, our editor-extraordinaire, thank you for everything throughout this process.

Next up, behind everything we put out at Mob, there is the amazing Mob team. So much work goes into the books that sits outside of the actual product. The promotion. The content. The marketing. The ongoing project management. This is all done by our brilliant team and I am so grateful to you all. A special thanks to Lucas for your contribution to the words of Fresh Mob.

And last but not least, some personal thanks. My family have been the ever-present source of reassurance and guidance since I launched Mob. Thank you Mum, Dad, Joe and Sam. I love you so much. And thank you to my girlfriend Robyn, the rock by my side.

Ben x

About Mob

Mob's mission is to help students and young professionals get more comfortable in the kitchen and make quality meals along the way. We're not about garnishes of micro herbs or "artistic" smears of sauces. We're all about accessibility and making things as simple and fun as possible when it comes to cooking.

Think of us like the friend you go to for brilliant restaurant recommendations or that one family member you've got that really knows their way around the kitchen. That's us.

The aim is to inspire and educate our audience through diverse and high-quality content, connecting the youth through what they love (and know) the most: food.

With multiple bestselling cookbooks already in the bag, Mob also has a strong social media presence on Instagram, Facebook, and TikTok. Give us a follow to keep up-to-date with our latest recipes.

First published in Great Britain in 2022 by Hodder & Stoughton
An Hachette UK company

1

A CIP catalogue record for this title is available from the British Library

Hardback ISBN 9781399705059
eBook ISBN 9781399705066

Editorial Director: Carolyn Thorne
Project Editor: Isabel Gonzalez-Prendergast
Copyeditor: Clare Sayer
Art Direction: Studio NARI
Layout Design: Nicky Barneby
Photography: David Loftus
Food Stylist: Elena Silcock
Props Stylist: Charlie Phillips
Senior Production Controller: Rachel Southey

Colour origination by Alta London
Printed and bound in Germany by Mohn Media

Hodder & Stoughton policy is to use papers that are natural, renewable and recyclable products and made from wood grown in sustainable forests. The logging and manufacturing processes are expected to conform to the environmental regulations of the country of origin.

Hodder & Stoughton Ltd
Carmelite House
50 Victoria Embankment
London
EC4Y 0DZ

www.hodder.co.uk